e **NAVY**

FIRST IN
THE FIGHT—
ALWAYS
FAITHFUL~
BE A U.S.MARINE!

JOIN THE
AIR SERVICE
and
SERVE
in
FRANCE

DO IT
NOW

I WANT YOU
FOR U.S. ARMY
NEAREST RECRUITING STATION

AMERICAN HERITAGE
ILLUSTRATED HISTORY
OF THE UNITED STATES

With German prisoners of war and American soldiers everywhere, the traffic to and from Mont St. Père is in a state of chaos, as the Allied counteroffensive drives a spearhead into the Marne salient on July 23, 1918.
SMITHSONIAN INSTITUTION

FRONT COVER: *An American doughboy stands atop a street barricade in war torn Chateau-Thierry in a detail of a watercolor by William J. Aylard, an Allied Expeditionary Force artist.*
SMITHSONIAN INSTITUTION

FRONT ENDSHEET: *Posters came into their own as powerful weapons in World War I.*
SUBMARINE LIBRARY; GENERAL DYNAMICS CORPORATION; FRANKLIN D. ROOSEVELT LIBRARY; MARINE CORPS MUSEUM; SMITHSONIAN INSTITUTION; WEST POINT MUSEUM

CONTENTS PAGE: *Howard Chandler Christy painted this poster for a bond drive.*
SMITHSONIAN INSTITUTION

BACK ENDSHEET: *Old songs and magazines recall World War I and the Jazz Age.*
CULVER PICTURES, NEW YORK PUBLIC LIBRARY

BACK COVER: *Surrounded by rubble, a doughboy (top) stands over the body of a dead comrade and fires at the enemy in Harvey Dunn's painting of street combat in France; Charles A. Lindbergh (bottom left) won world acclaim with his 1927 solo fight to France; Woodrow Wilson (bottom right) is the archetype of the idealist whose most cherished plans are frustrated by the realities of politics. Sir William Orpen painted him in 1919.*
SMITHSONIAN INSTITUTION; UNDERWOOD & UNDERWOOD; COLLECTION OF BERNARD BARUCH, JR.

AMERICAN HERITAGE
ILLUSTRATED HISTORY
OF THE UNITED STATES

VOLUME 13

WORLD WAR I

BY ROBERT G. ATHEARN

Created in Association with the
Editors of AMERICAN HERITAGE

and for the updated edition
MEDIA PROJECTS INCORPORATED

CHOICE PUBLISHING, INC.

New York

Library of Congress Catalog Card Number: 87-73399
ISBN 0-945260-13-X

This 1988 edition is published and distributed by Choice Publishing, Inc., 53 Watermill Lane, Great Neck, NY 11021
by arrangement with American Heritage, a division of Forbes, Inc.

Manufactured in the United States of America

CONTENTS OF THE COMPLETE SERIES

Editor's Note to the Revised Edition
Introduction by ALLAN NEVINS
Main text by ROBERT G. ATHEARN

EACH VOLUME CONTAINS AN ENCYCLOPEDIC SECTION; MASTER INDEX IN VOLUME 18

CONTENTS OF VOLUME 13

CHAPTER 37

THE GREAT CRUSADE

A little more than a year after Woodrow Wilson's inauguration, an event took place in Europe that was not only to destroy the uneasy peace there, but eventually to involve an isolationist America in a conflict from which it would emerge the leading power in the world. The nations of Europe were split into two major groups, between which a balance of power existed. On one side was the Triple Entente—France, Great Britain, and Russia; on the other, the Triple Alliance—Germany, Austria-Hungary, and (until 1915) Italy—also called the Central Powers. On June 28, 1914, Archduke Francis Ferdinand of Austria, heir to the throne of aged Emperor Francis Joseph, was assassinated at Sarajevo by a Serbian nationalist. At first, it appeared that this Balkan crisis might simmer down, but a month later, Austria severed relations with Serbia, a move that preceded war by only a few days. Ger-

Woodrow Wilson is the archetype of the idealist whose most cherished plans are frustrated by the realities of politics. Sir William Orpen painted him in 1919.

many backed Austria; Russia stepped forward to defend its small Balkan friend; and despite all efforts by would-be peacemakers to localize the dispute, France, Belgium, and soon Great Britain were involved. Almost overnight, Europe was at war.

American relations with European nations were at that time generally friendly, especially with Great Britain. But Wilson quickly called upon his countrymen to take no sides and to be "impartial in thought as well as action." The suggestion, admired as a theory, was largely ignored by the man on the street. Millions of "hyphenated" Americans—German-Americans, Irish-Americans, and others of foreign extraction—remembered the old country and had the normal sympathies toward their respective homelands. Even the governments abroad did not believe that Wilson would long honor his own words. Sir Cecil Spring-Rice, British ambassador to the United States, remarked that he was sure Wilson had "an understanding heart." The diplomat was right. Even though Wilson stated his desire for neutrality in a public declaration on August 19, 1914,

The assassination of Austrian Archduke Francis Ferdinand in June, 1914, caused a Balkan crisis that grew into World War I.

the American government soon began to show sympathy for the Allies (as the Entente governments came to be called) in their struggle against the Central Powers.

Friendship and neutrality are hard to combine in wartime. British complaints against alleged German breaches of international law made matters particularly difficult for Wilson. There was sharp pressure from private banking firms for permission to loan money to the Allies. Officially,

Wilson frowned upon the practice, but before the year 1914 was out, the City Bank of New York had loaned the French government $10,000,000. When peace-minded Congressmen expressed a desire to create an arms embargo, thus shutting off supplies to the Allies, the administration repudiated the idea. Meanwhile, American farmers and manufacturers protested any restrictions on international trade. Cotton farmers saw an opportunity to capitalize upon the war and overcome a downward trend in prices. The South, a Democratic stronghold, had to be considered. In short, Wilson the idealist once again found himself confronted with realities and was obliged to retreat before the barrage of economic demands. Before long, his administration had to take the position that Americans could sell goods or loan money to any foreign country. It was a concession filled with risks, and Wilson knew it.

As the war went on, American involvement deepened. Walter Hines Page, United States ambassador to London, was outspoken in his belief that America should enter the war against Germany. When Wilson tried to tone him down, Page became uncooperative to the point of giving the British information he should have kept secret. The ambassador's attitude, supported by expressions of friendship from other Americans, encouraged the British to believe they could push their control of the world's shipping lanes even to the point of

"All the News That's Fit to Print."

The New York Times.

THE WEATHER
Fair today and Sunday, fresh to strong southwest to west winds.
For full weather report see Page 3.

VOL. LXIV...NO. 20,923. .. NEW YORK, SATURDAY, MAY 8, 1915.—TWENTY-FOUR PAGES. ONE CENT In Greater New York, Jersey City and Newark. | Elsewhere TWO CENTS.

LUSITANIA SUNK BY A SUBMARINE, PROBABLY 1,000 DEAD; TWICE TORPEDOED OFF IRISH COAST; SINKS IN 15 MINUTES; AMERICANS ABOARD INCLUDED VANDERBILT AND FROHMAN; WASHINGTON BELIEVES THAT A GRAVE CRISIS IS AT HAND

SHOCKS THE PRESIDENT

Washington Deeply Stirred by Disaster and Fears a Crisis.

BULLETINS AT WHITE HOUSE

Wilson Reads Them Closely, but Is Silent on the Nation's Course.

HINTS OF CONGRESS CALL

Loss of Lusitania Recalls Firm Tone of Our First Warning to Germany.

CAPITAL FULL OF RUMORS

Reports That Liner Was to be Sunk Were Heard Before Actual News Came.

Special to The New York Times.

WASHINGTON, May 7.—Never since that April day, three years ago, when word came that the Titanic had gone down, has Washington been so stirred as it is tonight over the sinking of the Lusitania. The early reports told that there had been no loss of life, but the relief that these advices caused gave way to the greatest concern late this evening when it became known that there had been many deaths. Although they are profoundly reticent, officials realize that this tragedy, involving the loss of American citizens, is likely to bring about a crisis in the international relations of the United States.

It is pointed out that the sinking of the Lusitania is the outcome of a series of incidents that have been the

The Lost Cunard Steamship Lusitania
X Where the First Torpedo Struck. XX Where the Second Torpedo Struck.

Cunard Office Here Besieged for News; Fate of 1,918 on Lusitania Long in Doubt

Fate of Most of the Well-Known Passengers Still in Doubt —Story of Disaster Long Unconfirmed While Anxious Crowds Seek Details.

Roosevelt Calls It Piracy; Says That We Must Act.

Special to The New York Times.

SYRACUSE, N. Y., May 7.—Ex-President Roosevelt, after learning details of the

Meagre List of Saved Received in New York

Those whose rescue was reported to New York by Cable by the Liverpool offices of the Cunard Line and

Loss of the Lusitania Fills London With Horror and Utter Amazement

News Held Back for Hours—Anxious Crowds Wait All Night at Steamship Offices for Word of Friends and Relatives.

SOME DEAD TAKEN ASHORE

Several Hundred Survivors at Queenstown and Kinsale.

STEWARD TELLS OF DISASTER

One Torpedo Crashes Into the Doomed Liner's Bow, Another Into the Engine Room.

SHIP LISTS OVER TO PORT

Makes It Impossible to Lower Many Boats, So Hundreds Must Have Gone Down.

ATTACKED IN BROAD DAY

Passengers at Luncheon—Warning Had Been Given by Germans Before the Ship Left New York.

LONDON, Saturday, May 8.—The Cunard liner Lusitania, which sailed out of New York last Saturday with 1,918 souls aboard, lies at the bottom of the ocean off the Irish coast. She was sunk by a German submarine, which sent two torpedoes crashing into her side at 2:30 o'clock yesterday afternoon while the passengers, seemingly confident that the great, swift vessel could elude the German underwater craft, were having luncheon.

The great inrush of water caused the liner to list heavily to port, so that she could not launch many of her lifeboat

---

The New York Times *stated that the* Lusitania *had been "twice torpedoed" on May 7, 1915. It was hit only once; then an internal explosion followed.*

---

stepping on neutral toes. Attempting to cope with the growing dilemma, Wilson talked at length with his closest adviser, Colonel Edward M. House. He read to the colonel from *The History of the American* by Professor Woodrow Wilson, pointing out that the War of 1812 had grown from a similar situation. Historian Wilson remarked that he and James Madison were the only two Princeton men to become President, and that the circumstances they faced in international

war had, so far, run parallel. This was as far as he wanted the comparison to go; he had to avoid involvement.

The Germans, too, objected to British methods. On February 4, 1915, they proclaimed the waters around the British Isles a war zone and said they would sink all enemy ships found there. Also, they told neutrals to stay away, as the British were guilty of misusing a neutral flag to disguise their own ships. Germany had a point. Colonel House, while traveling on the

1087

U-boats sank many British vessels in their tightened blockade of the islands in early 1917, crippling Britain's shipping and threatening the country with starvation.

British liner *Lusitania* in February, 1915, was surprised to see the American flag run up as the vessel approached the Irish coast. When the United States remonstrated, the British argued that the Germans ought to stop any ships whose identity they doubted. Both sides knew this was impractical, as German submarines, or U-boats, would not surface and risk being shot out of the water by a deck gun. Nonetheless, Wilson protested the submarine blockade of the British Isles and warned against the sinking of any American ships.

In a desperate war, the neutral always runs a heavy risk. It was true in the Napoleonic Wars and it was true in Wilson's day. On March 28, 1915, the first American life was lost in the sinking of the British ship *Falaba*. A month later, German airplanes attacked the American steamship *Cushing,* and on May 1, the American tanker *Gulflight* was torpedoed. That same day, the *Lusitania* sailed from New York carrying American passengers who had ignored the German embassy's warnings. A week later, as she approached the Irish coast, the *Lusitania* was topedoed and sunk with the loss of 1,198 lives, including 128 Americans. From New York to San Francisco the press condemned this "slaughter," "wholesale murder," and "piracy" by the Ger-mans. Colonel House predicted we would be at war within a month.

Despite a German apology, and the revelation that the *Lusitania* carried military supplies and 4,200 cases of cartridges, the incident had a profound effect on both the American people and the administration. Continued sinkings kept public anger high. In the spring of 1916, the French steamer *Sussex* was torpedoed, injuring some of her American passengers. As

Germany had agreed not to sink unarmed passenger vessels without warning, Wilson got from the Germans what he regarded as a promise to modify their conduct. This *"Sussex* pledge" was to be used as a test of Germany's sincerity. For nine months it was kept.

Apparently satisfied, Wilson ran for re-election in 1916, with "He kept us out of war" as his supporters' best slogan. Although Charles Evans Hughes, the Republican candidate, made it a close race, Wilson won. The following January, Germany again tightened its blockade on the British Isles and announced it would sink all suspicious ships. Wilson regarded the renewal of unrestricted submarine warfare as a violation of the *Sussex* pledge. His desire to be neutral was further weakened when, late in February, he learned that the German foreign secretary,

THE NAVY NEEDS YOU! DON'T **READ** AMERICAN HISTORY— **MAKE IT!**

U·S·NAVY RECRUITING STATION
34 E. 23rd St., N.Y. & 23 N. Broadway, Yonkers, N.Y.

This recruiting poster hoped to make white-collar stay-at-homes eager for adventure.

Arthur Zimmermann, had cabled his minister at Mexico City to make an alliance with Mexico in case of war with America. The minister was to promise the Mexicans the return of New Mexico, Arizona, and Texas and was to try to persuade the Mexican president to invite the Japanese into the alliance. Zimmermann's note, intercepted by British intelligence, was turned over to Ambassador Page, who sent it to the State Department. News of the Zimmermann proposal was released to the public in March,

the same month that three American ships were attacked without warning and sunk. Wilson decided to ask Congress to recognize that a state of war existed between the United States and Germany. On April 6, 1917, the resolution had passed both houses. Wilson signed it, and America's neutrality ended. Wilson the peaceful, Wilson the idealist was now a war President.

A democracy goes to war

If America were going to fight a total war, every bit of available manpower would have to be tapped. Men had volunteered in greater numbers than the army could use during the Spanish-American War, but the present conflict was different. Not only was the enemy far away and much more formidable, but young men were no longer so eager for glory. For several years they had read of mud and blood in the trenches of France, and they found little glamour in the idea of fighting against tanks, machine guns, and poison gas.

Clearly the volunteer system would not work. The answer was conscription, which would provide not only the necessary manpower but would allow the government to draw on it in an equitable manner. Knowing the traditional American antipathy toward the draft, and remembering the bitter riots it had caused during the Civil War, Wilson tried to minimize the complaints he knew would come. Thus the government arranged that young men be inducted by boards

American destroyers arrived at Queenstown, Ireland, in May, 1917, to help hunt down German submarines that were fast cutting off transport to England.

made up of people from their own communities.

Quietly the administration prepared its conscription bill, and on May 18, 1917, it became law—although Speaker of the House Champ Clark claimed there was "precious little difference between conscript and convict." On June 5, more than 9,-000,000 men, between the ages of 21 and 30, registered for service.

In the prewar years, Wilson had been criticized for his failure to prepare the country for possible involvement. Now his administration pushed mobilization with every resource at its command. Army camps began to dot the land, and civilian contractors fought with one another for lumber, steel, plumbing supplies, and all other materials necessary to build them. Food, bedding, clothing, and innumerable additional requirements for an army of several million had to be procured, and ships had to be built to carry them across the ocean.

America also had to produce new weapons, for the advances in armaments since 1914 had outmoded much of the equipment already owned by the army and navy. There was such a shortage in artillery, and what existed was so antiquated, that for heavy ordnance America would rely chiefly upon guns supplied by the French and British. There was no national aircraft industry. When the United States went to war, its air arm (then part of the army) had but 55 airplanes, all of them obsolete; most American pilots flew in craft either designed or built by the Allies.

"Over there"

The apparent indifference of the Germans to America's entry into the war represented a gamble. Although well aware of the potential power of the newest belligerent, the planners at Berlin were confident that their U-boats could starve out the British Isles before the slow-moving trans-atlantic democracy could get an army in the field.

It was a great risk, but in 1917 the odds seemed to be in their favor. From January to June, submarines sank 2,275,000 tons of British shipping and 1,580,000 tons of Allied and neutral shipping. Both sides knew that if this rate increased, the Allies would be in serious difficulty, for ships could not be built as fast as they were being sunk. The only hope the Allies had was to improve their antisubmarine methods. In the second half of 1917,

Surrounded by rubble, a doughboy stands over the body of a dead comrade and fires at the enemy in Harvey Dunn's painting of street combat in France.

the use of convoys and depth charges cut shipping losses almost in half, and in the early months of 1918, it appeared that the Germans had miscalculated their ability to isolate the British Isles.

A second miscalculation was the belief that America would be slow in mobilizing her tremendous resources. Not only was a Selective Service Act passed within a few weeks after Wilson signed the war resolution, but Congress also quickly enacted legislation authorizing two Liberty Loan drives and soldiers' and sailors' insurance; controlling aviation, food, and fuel; increasing taxes; setting more severe punishment for espionage; and forbidding trading with the enemy. By October, appropriations totaling almost $19,000,000,000 had been approved. For the Allies, however, America's war effort was all too slow. Not until October was any of the American Expeditionary Force at the front, and then only token detachments stationed in quiet sectors. By the end of 1917, perhaps 250,000 American servicemen were in France, most of them still in advanced training. General John J. Pershing, commander in chief of the A.E.F., asked for 1,000,000 men in France by the end of May, 1918, but by March had only 500,000.

Even more distressing to the Allies was the quarrel with the American military over how the expeditionary force would be used. Pershing insisted upon a separate American

General John J. "Black Jack" Pershing, commander in chief of the American Expeditionary Force in Europe, refused to integrate his divisions with other Allied troops.

army; the French and British wanted to integrate the newly arrived troops with their own as quickly as possible. Pershing was deaf to pleas that Germany might win before his troops got into action, and that as both American officers and men were untested in battle, it was unwise to entrust a whole sector of the front to inexperienced divisions. The argument grew so acrimonious that England's Prime Minister David Lloyd George and French Premier Georges Clemenceau went over Pershing's head and appealed to Woodrow Wilson. But the President stood firmly behind his general.

The early months of 1918 marked the high point of the war for Germany. A revolution-torn Russia had been beaten decisively, and in March, 1918, the new Bolshevik leaders gave in to the harsh terms imposed by the Germans in the Treaty of Brest-Litovsk, thus ending the war on the eastern front. Freed from this commitment, and now able to transfer vast numbers of men to the west, the Germans prepared a mighty series of offensives aimed at crushing the British and French before the Americans arrived.

On March 21, 1918, three German armies numbering well over 800,000 men struck the British along a 40-mile front, and within two days, British Field Marshal Douglas Haig's outnumbered troops were in full retreat. As the British swung back toward the Channel, ready to evacuate by sea, they opened a gap between themselves and the French forces. But before the Germans could exploit it, the French sent reinforcements, and the Allied line held. During the spring of 1918, the Germans continued to hammer at the Allied defenses. Again and again they made spectacular gains, only to be stopped short of a truly decisive victory. By summer, however, great numbers of Americans were ready to fight, and it became apparent that the German gamble had failed.

In mid-July, the German commander, Erich von Ludendorff, made his final effort, launching an attack in the Marne Valley aimed at Paris. This struggle was the turning point of the war—for here the exhausted Germans were halted once and for all, and an Allied counteroffensive began. Now there were 1,000,000 Americans in France, and another 500,000 would arrive before November. Using American troops to spearhead the drive in the Marne salient, the Allies pushed the German armies back; soon a general attack was mounted all along the western front. Although the Germans put up a stiff resistance, their fight was hopeless. By fall, with their armies in collapse and revolution threatening at home, they willingly agreed to an armistice. Thus, on November 11, 1918, World War I came to an end.

If American aid was late, it came when most needed. It boosted Allied morale when at its lowest ebb. In an almost continuous series of battles, American troops captured nearly 45,-000 prisoners, took some 1,400 guns, and brought down over 700 enemy aircraft. Over 50,000 Americans died in battle, a slight figure compared to the losses of the Allies, who had been fighting more than four years. Active American participation had lasted no more than a few months.

The home front

At home, noncombatants made their contribution, too. In mobilizing civilians, Wilson had three able assistants—Newton D. Baker, Secretary of War; Bernard M. Baruch, chairman of the War Industries Board; and George Creel, head of the Committee on Public Information. Creel and Baruch were performing tasks with-

The air full of poison gas, the Marine Brigade of the Second Division at the Battle of Belleau Wood fights through its grim 19-day engagement.

out precedent in American history, and their orders were often criticized.

Baruch had the problem of running all American industry as if it were a single factory. For example, the War Industries Board decided that 8,000 tons of steel a year was too much to allot to women's corsets, and it stop-ped the manufacture of them. Then, to avoid hurting a civilian industry, the board let corset manufacturers make masks and belts for the Army Medical Corps. So it was in other industries. Women's blouse factories made signal flags, radiator manufacturers made guns, automobile factories

Tanks manned by American soldiers slowly make their way up a hill to go into battle with the Germans near Bourevilles, France, on September 26, 1918.

made airplane engines, and piano companies made airplane wings.

Labor was a key segment of the civilian army. Wages of industrial workers rose so fast that inflation resulted, causing a wave of potentially crippling strikes by the fall of 1917. Workers rightly claimed that their real wages were diminishing as prices went up. To stop the spiral, the government formed the National War Labor Board, with ex-President Taft and labor lawyer Frank Walsh at its head. Companies flouting its decisions were taken over by the government. And when workers became unreasonable, they were threatened with induction into the armed services, a device that was usually effective.

Although the government was obliged to take over some industries as a punitive measure, it did so with others for greater efficiency. In December, 1917, the government assumed control of all major railroads, under the Secretary of the Treasury, William G. McAdoo. The railroads complained that their rolling stock was being mishandled or allowed to deteriorate, that government concessions to labor would make postwar labor-management problems more difficult, and that federal operation would decrease the general efficiency of the lines, but their outcries were lost in the general din of mobilization.

As always in wartime, there were shortages. To make the maximum use of fuel, so necessary to manufacturers and military alike, a fuel administrator was appointed. Marshal Fer-dinand Foch of France issued a grim warning to the United States: "If you don't keep up your oil supply, we shall lose the war." But in a day when natural gas was not available in quantity across the land, coal was just as important to both homes and factories, and with the demands of the war, it was becoming increasingly

The chaos of war is everywhere on a road at Esnes, France, on September 29, 1918, as American troops push their way to the front in the Meuse-Argonne offensive.

scarce. As a crisis mounted in the winter of 1917–18, Fuel Administrator Harry A. Garfield, former president of Williams College, ordered that industrial plants east of the Mississippi River be shut down on Mondays until the end of March. Offices, stores, schools, and places of amusement also had their coal supply sharply curtailed. Civilians were asked to observe "heatless Monday" and to "save a shovelful of coal a day." To save gasoline and oil, they were urged to do less pleasure driving by observing "gasless Sunday."

An administration to conserve food was set up, headed by Herbert Hoover. As European demand for foodstuffs increased, Americans had to tighten their belts; as Wilson put it, they were "now eating at a common table." The Allies particularly needed fats and sugar. To aid them, Americans sharply reduced their own use of sugar and pork, while farmers made every effort to raise more pigs. As one commentator wrote, "The American hog became an exalted animal, commanding for the moment a rather more intent regard than the lion or the eagle; the hog population was almost as much a concern to the government as manpower."

Finally, a huge propaganda campaign was mounted on the home front. George Creel's Committee on Public Information employed any and all who could transmit ideas—singers, painters, sculptors, illustrators, designers, and cartoonists. The country was literally plastered with posters—in streetcars, on billboards, on barn walls, along highways, and in all public buildings. Volunteer "Four-Minute Men" stood up in lodge meetings, dining clubs, schools, union meetings, and even in lumber camps to give their brief but urgent message. Tin Pan Alley did its share also, producing *Over There, Goodbye Broadway,*

As in all war propaganda, the enemy in 1918 became the symbol of everything that was ruthless, destructive, and horrifying.

Hello France, and a host of other tuneful reminders that a world war was in progress.

By November 11, 1918, it was, as George M. Cohan's popular song said, "over, over there." A little more than three weeks later, the American liner *George Washington* sailed for Europe carrying President Wilson. The former college professor broke a tradition, for he was the first American chief executive to visit Europe, or any foreign land, while in office. His was a mission of peace and personal diplomacy, a continuation of his crusade to make the world "safe for democracy." It was a journey widely heralded by the ordinary folk of Europe, who were much impressed by Wilson's idealism and his hopes for the future. Italians put his picture in the windows of their homes and many a peasant burned candles before it. Ray Stannard Baker related that university men in Poland used his name as a greeting, crying out "Wilson!" when they met and shook hands. Paris eagerly awaited his coming, and the city was decorated with banners bearing the words "Honor to Wilson the Just." There was a general, if undefined, feeling that the tall, sober American could heal all the earth's long-festering sores. With him he brought proposals for settlements, some of which were not even related to the Allied or Central powers, or even to the recent war.

It was Wilson's hope that a peace settlement could be made on the basis

The home front was mobilized by posters like this one exhorting people to plant war gardens and can their vegetables—and so "can" the German Kaiser, Wilhelm II, too.

of the Fourteen Points he had laid before Congress early in 1918. Principally they had called for freedom of the seas; the end of secret diplomacy and artificial trade barriers; arms reduction; a settlement of colonial claims; German evacuation of Russia, Belgium, and France; the redrawing of national boundaries and self-determination for all people. The 14th, and most widely discussed, point suggested a general association, or league, of nations to guarantee political freedom to all nations, large and small alike.

American liberals enthusiastically accepted the idealistic aims of the Fourteen Points and, as long as the war lasted, the Allied powers appeared to share their feelings. Once the peace talks opened in Paris on January 18, 1919, however, the victorious European nations began to make specific territorial or financial demands that did not always fit the pattern of Wilson's more general proposals. The very size of the gathering created great difficulties. The British delegation filled five hotels, and at one time the Americans, ranging from high diplomats to clerks, numbered 1,300. It soon became apparent that a few of the leaders would have to make most of the decisions if any solutions were to be reached.

Wilson led the United States delegation; Premier Clemenceau and Marshal Foch represented France; Prime Minister David Lloyd George headed the British group; and Premier Vittorio Orlando spoke for the Italians.

The horror of war is reflected in the gaunt faces of the German prisoners (at the center) and the wounded American soldiers, who stream back from the front during the Meuse-Argonne fighting of 1918.

No Germans were present at the preliminary sessions, for the Allies had long since decided to deny the vanquished any voice in the drafting of the treaty. They intended neither to listen to arguments from the Germans nor to haggle with them.

From January to May, the representatives worked at various problems, assembling details, searching for solutions. Directing the work was the Supreme Council, made up of two delegates apiece from the United States, Great Britain, France, Italy, and Japan. When this group proved to be somewhat unwieldy, it was reduced from 10 to five delegates. Then Japan, which had played a relatively small role in the war, was dropped. After complaining that Italy was not getting all she had been promised, Orlando went home. This left only the Big Three to do the treaty-making.

The treaty

As Wilson, Clemenceau, and Lloyd George fashioned the general outline of the treaty, it became increasingly clear that most of Wilson's idealistic plans would be disregarded. The European members of the group were fully aware that Wilson's great dream was a League of Nations, and although they were in general agreement that an organization of this kind was necessary, they also saw in the President's obsession a chance to gain concessions for their own countries. France demanded maximum protection against future aggressions by Germany, and with British support, she asked for reparations that would cripple her former enemy economically for years to come. For their part, the British objected to reducing armaments, because it would mean reducing the size of their navy, then the greatest in the world. The Italians were much upset by Wilson's refusal to grant them territory promised in the secret Treaty of London four years earlier. The Belgians, too, were dissatisfied and threatened to boycott the sessions. At this point, the Japanese demanded Germany's former rights in the Chinese Shantung Peninsula, asserting that they had been promised to them. When Wilson yielded, he alienated the Chinese, who subsequently refused to sign the treaty. To cap it all, American-Irish groups said Wilson was not working hard enough for Irish independence and denounced him as a British puppet. On the other hand, Clemenceau thought he was pro-German, while the Italians accused him of favoring their rivals, the Yugoslavs. The President was also sharply attacked at home by Republican protectionists in the Senate for his desire to eliminate economic trade barriers.

After long and acrimonious arguments, in which Wilson often re-treated to ward off further attacks upon his cherished league, a treaty was drawn up. The signing took place at Versailles on June 28, 1919, the fifth anniversary of the assassination of the Austrian Archduke Francis Ferdinand. Germany was ordered to agree to a document that not only fixed guilt for the war upon her but directed her to pay its entire cost. Even Wilson the Just did not object to the terms. "I believe," he said in defense of his stand, "that a hard peace is a good thing for Germany herself, in order that she may know what an unjust war means."

Whether it was a good or a just treaty, it did not provide a lasting peace. It was sharply criticized by the liberals of the time, because too many of Wilson's Fourteen Points had been lost. To be sure, such doctrines as the self-determination of peoples appeared in the treaty, but even this laudable idea was badly distorted in the whittling-down and compromising. Although the treaty had limitations in its attempts to arrive at settlements, its greatest weakness lay in the economic penalties levied on the German nation. Had these strictures been less harsh, there would have been less reason for the discontent that paved the way for Adolf Hitler's rise a few years later. If the price demanded had not been so unrealistically high, the German people might have been willing to attempt to pay it. But the bill charged them totaled more than the value of the entire gold supply in the

The victorious war leaders met in Paris in 1919 for a settlement of the massive conflict—(left to right) Lloyd George, Orlando, Clemenceau, and Wilson.

world at that time. To make it worse, when Germany tried to pay off her debt by trading with such countries as the United States, high tariffs made it impossible. Thus it was not hard for rabble-rousers like Hitler to use the widespread hatred of the Versailles Treaty to win support.

Treaty wrecking in the Senate

During the months that Democrat Wilson labored at the Paris peace table, his Republican opponents in the Senate prepared their battle lines and awaited his return. They resented the fact that their party, which had gained control of the Senate in the 1918 elections, was practically ignored by the President, and they resolved to take their revenge when the treaty came up for ratification.

Had Wilson been less inflexible, he might have saved his League of Nations. During February, 1919, he made a short trip home from Paris to sign some bills and to consult with the Senate Foreign Relations Committee. Early the next month, 39 Senators and Senators-elect presented him with a statement to the effect that

1103

any discussion of the league should wait until a peace treaty was signed. The President flatly refused to consider the idea.

Led by Senators William Borah of Idaho and Henry Cabot Lodge of Massachusetts, a small group of "irreconcilables" determined to kill the league, even if they had to reject the entire treaty in the process. But Wilson's opponents needed time to organize their forces. First they insisted that all 264 pages of the document be read before the Senate. This took two weeks. Then came six more weeks of public hearings. During this period, the treaty opponents enlisted the aid of such wealthy men as Henry Clay Frick and Andrew Mellon, whose money financed a massive propaganda attack throughout the nation.

While speakers launched their attacks in public places, the treaty wreckers in the Senate, led by Lodge, went to work in earnest. By September, 1919, the Foreign Relations Committee reported that it had added 45 amendments and four reservations. When Congress voted them down, Lodge's committee came right back with additional reservations, the most important of which was a provision that the United States had no obligation to protect the territorial integrity or political independence of any other nation.

Meanwhile, the grave, introspective schoolmaster in the White House was not willing to stand by and watch his creation ripped to pieces. Tired and worn from his nerve-racking trials at the peace conference, he still somehow found the strength to fight back; it would prove the final battle of his life. His eloquent pleas before the Senate had been received coldly as "glittering generalities" and "soap bubbles of oratory." Now he had no choice but to carry his crusade to the ultimate source of power—the voters.

In the fall of 1919, he undertook a journey that carried him across the nation—8,000 miles in 22 days—during which he delivered 37 long addresses. But on September 25, at Pueblo, Colorado, exhaustion overcame him, and in a state of near collapse he returned quickly to Washington. A week later, he was stricken with a near-fatal paralytic stroke.

During November, as Wilson lay ill, the Senators concluded their vivisection of the treaty. The irreconcilables managed to attach 15 reservations and so burdened it that there was no possibility of the necessary two-thirds vote for ratification. In an effort to put an official end to America's participation in the war, Congress in May, 1920, adopted a joint resolution repealing the declaration of war against the Central Powers. Still pressing for acceptance of his version of the treaty, Wilson vetoed it. There the matter stood until Warren G. Harding was inaugurated. In July, 1921, he signed the resolution, and in this vacillating way America formally ended its part in the "great crusade."

U.S. AIR FORCE

THE WAR IN THE AIR

When World War I began in 1914, France had a relatively large air force—260 planes—and 191 trained pilots. Germany had a mere 46 planes, England only 29. None of these were armed, and it was assumed that they would be used solely for observation. Soon, however, the rival pilots took to firing pistols and rifles at one another as they passed in the air. Then the Frenchman Roland Garros put metal deflectors on his propeller so he could use a forward-firing machine gun without splintering the propeller. Next, a Dutchman named Anthony Fokker, who was working for Germany, invented a synchronizing gear that permitted a machine gun to fire only when the propeller was not in the way, and a truly efficient system of making war in the air had been found. Planes could now strafe enemy troops and shoot down enemy aircraft to prevent observation. There were some primitive attempts at bombing, but in the early days it was generally the single-seater pursuit ship against another single-seater or an observation plane, as above: French ace Georges Guynemer in his Spad has just shot down a German two-seater carrying pilot and observer.

Oswald Boelcke (above, left) used Fokker's synchronizing gear and became Germany's first ace with 40 kills before he crashed in October, 1916. The Fokker he is flying was the finest fighter of 1915—capable of the then-amazing 93 miles per hour.

A wounded flyer (below) hangs over the rim of his cockpit while his mate pilots the plane home. This craft was called a "pusher" because the propeller was in the rear. The design with the engine behind the pilot had a brief popularity during 1914–15.

THE KNIGHTS OF THE SKY

Baron Manfred von Richthofen, the Red Knight of Germany, had 80 victories, the largest score made by any pilot on either side during the war, before Canadian Captain Roy Brown got on the tail of the baron's Fokker triplane and, perhaps assisted by Australian ground-fire (above, right), shot him down on April 21, 1918, with a bullet in the chest.

OVERLEAF: A pilot of the Lafayette Escadrille begins a strafing run. The squadron was formed in April, 1916, and it included seven young Americans who had volunteered with the French. Eventually, 38 Americans flew with the famous Indian-head unit.

U.S. AIR FORCE

FAMOUS AIRPLANES: 1914–1918

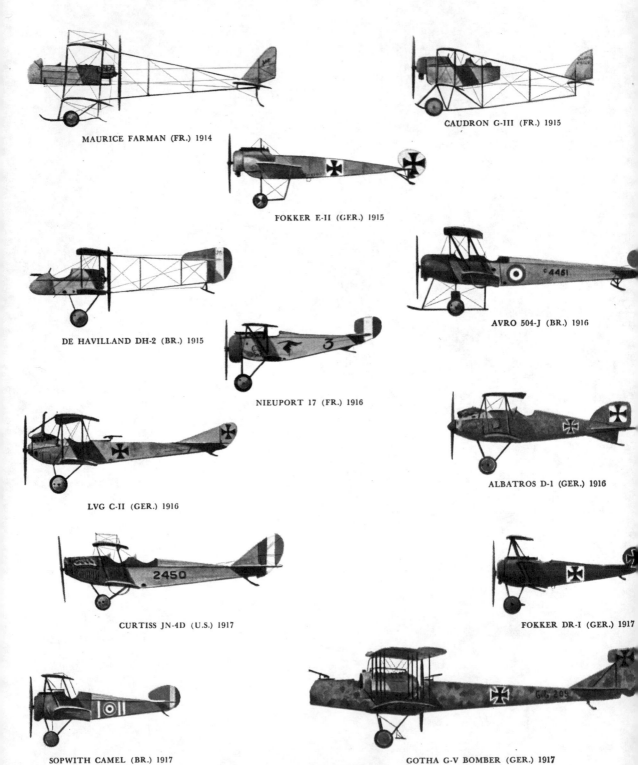

MAURICE FARMAN (FR.) 1914

CAUDRON G-III (FR.) 1915

FOKKER E-II (GER.) 1915

DE HAVILLAND DH-2 (BR.) 1915

AVRO 504-J (BR.) 1916

NIEUPORT 17 (FR.) 1916

LVG C-II (GER.) 1916

ALBATROS D-1 (GER.) 1916

CURTISS JN-4D (U.S.) 1917

FOKKER DR-I (GER.) 1917

SOPWITH CAMEL (BR.) 1917

GOTHA G-V BOMBER (GER.) 1917

BRISTOL F-2B (BR.) 1917

SPAD 13 (FR.) 1917

BREGUET 14 (FR.) 1917

SE-5 (BR.) 1917

FOKKER D-VII (GER.) 1918

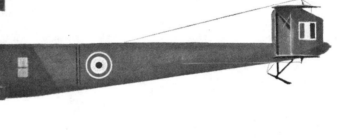

HANDLEY PAGE 0/400 (BR.) 1917

JUNKERS D-I (GER.) 1918

AMERICAN DH-4 (BR.-U.S.) 1918

LOENING M-8 (U.S.) 1918

NAVY-CURTISS F-5L (U.S.) 1918

THE WAR IN THE AIR

TERROR RAIDS
ON LONDON

In January, 1915, the German Naval Airship Division began to bomb London by zeppelin, and the British retaliated with barrage balloons (below). Lieutenant Reginald Warneford won the Victoria Cross by dropping six 20-pound bombs on an enemy craft (right) and setting her afire.

1113

"BOMBS AWAY"

When the zeppelins failed, the Germans bombed England with Gotha bombers (above).
Although they carried 1,500 pounds of bombs, they inflicted only slight damage in 52 raids.

The Allies tried bombing and spotting, with planes like the French Caudron (above), and night bombing (below) when antiaircraft losses made day raids too expensive. Not until 1918 did British General Hugh Trenchard receive permission for true strategic bombing—raids on German cities and factories.

BOELCKE

THE ACES

FONCK

NUNGESSER

BISHOP

MANNOCK

These were some of the leading pilots. From the top, left: Oswald Boelcke, German ace and teacher of aces; Rene Fonck, top French ace with 75 kills. Frenchman Charles Nungesser later died trying to fly the Atlantic. Canadian ace Billy Bishop shot down 72 planes; Edward "Mick" Mannock led the English with 73 victories. The American Frank Luke was an expert at knocking down German observation balloons. Manfred von Richthofen is shown with members of his Flying Circus. Eddie Rickenbacker, top American ace, made 26 kills. He led the Hat in the Ring squadron.

RICHTHOFEN (top, center)

LUKE

RICKENBACKER

CHAPTER 38

THE BUSINESSMAN'S GOVERNMENT

Johnny came marching home from the trenches to a country tired of sacrifice and idealism. Amid the confusion of returning to a peacetime economy and way of life, there grew a feeling of disillusion—a conviction that the expenditure of American blood and treasure on the battlefields of Europe had been for nothing. As the desire to make the world "safe for democracy" gave way to a quest for individual prosperity and security, people lost interest in foreign affairs. They began to feel nostalgic for the good old prewar days. President Warren G. Harding expressed it with the words "return to normalcy."

Nothing, in fact, demonstrated this longing for "normalcy" more than the election of the genial and innocuous Senator from Ohio. During 1920, as Americans made ready to choose a successor to the professor-President, Wilson, there was a desire, perhaps unconscious, to forget the crusades of the past eight years. The political tide

The Allies Day parade on New York's Fifth Avenue, painted by Childe Hassam, symbolizes Allied Unity when America entered World War I—a unity ending with the war.

was running Republican—a trend that had become apparent two years earlier after the G.O.P.'s victories in the 1918 Congressional elections.

By the time the Republican convention met at Chicago in June, party members were buoyantly confident. Flushed with their recent triumph over Wilson and the League of Nations, the conservatives took charge.

As it was probable that the Republican Party's nominee would be the next President, droves of candidates made their availability known. Perhaps the only person who seemed sure of the result was Harry M. Daugherty, a small-town Ohio lawyer. A man with considerable influence in the party in his home state, he predicted as early as February that the convention would arrive at a deadlock. Then, about two o'clock in the morning, Daugherty continued, "some 15 men, bleary-eyed with loss of sleep and perspiring profusely with the excessive heat, will sit down at a big table. I will be with them and will present the name of Senator Harding· to them, and before we get through, they will put him over." Harding was indeed "put over" in just that way. Governor

President Harding poses with his original cabinet—(seated, left to right) John W. Weeks, Andrew W. Mellon, Charles Evans Hughes, Harding, Vice-President Calvin Coolidge, Edwin Denby; (standing) Albert B. Fall, Will H. Hays, Harry M. Daugherty, Henry C. Wallace, Herbert Hoover, and J. J. Davis.

Calvin Coolidge of Massachusetts, whose one claim to national recognition had been his suppression of the Boston police strike in 1919, was nominated for the Vice-Presidency.

The unfavorable press reaction to the nomination gave the Democrats hope. One New York paper characterized Harding as "a very respectable Ohio politician of the second class" and his Senate record as "faint and colorless." And the Republicans produced a platform to match their candidate. The question of a League of Nations was handled so that it offended no one. Businessmen were wooed by promises to return the railroads and the merchant marine to private ownership and to give greater protection to manufacturers through tariff increases. The tendency of federal centralization, marked in the last years of the Wilson administration, was condemned.

The Democrats tried to capitalize upon Harding's weaknesses and upon Wilson's record. They nominated Governor James Cox of Ohio for President and Assistant Secretary of the Navy Franklin D. Roosevelt to run with him. The party promised to work for ratification of the peace treaty (although it did not oppose qualifying reservations), and to carry on the principles of Wilson's New Freedom. But neither the candidates nor their platforms had much appeal for the voters. Harding sat at home in Marion, Ohio, and let the public's desire for a change carry him to victory. On November 2, his 55th birthday, he was elected in a landslide, with 16,152,200 votes to 9,147,353 for Cox.

Harding's cabinet appointees were a measure of the lackluster quality of the man. In probably his best appointment, he made Charles Evans Hughes Secretary of State, mainly because, as he said, Hughes had been "approximately" elected President in 1916. Andrew Mellon, the Pittsburgh millionaire, headed the Treasury Department; Albert B. Fall of New Mexico became Secretary of the Interior; and as a reward for his efforts at the Republican convention, Harry Daugherty was made Attorney General. Except for Hughes, only the appointment of Henry C. Wallace as Secretary of Agriculture and Herbert Hoover as Secretary of Commerce added distinction to Harding's cabinet. A number of lesser government offices went to members of the "Ohio gang," as Harding's intimates were known.

Harding's normalcy

When Harding called for a return to normalcy, it was understood that he wanted to go back to the "good old days," but exactly how far back he did not say. Politically, he seemed to have returned his party—and the

The sidelined Democratic Party exults over the unsavory oil scandals in the administration of the Republican Harding.

Its attitude different from that in the previous cartoon, the Democratic Party joins the Republican Party in wishing the Senate would find a distraction.

nation—to the era of McKinley. High tariffs and hands off big business were the rule; the progressive politics of Roosevelt and Wilson were shunned like a bad memory. As for morals, Harding's administration, with its blight of fraud and corruption, seemed a throwback to General Grant's.

In the beginning, the nation suspected none of this. Harding was personally popular, and his friendly attitude toward business satisfied the conservative temper of the times. In at least one instance, the Washington Conference for the Limitation of Armament, which produced a treaty limiting the naval armaments of the major powers, the administration could boast a significant, if regrettably short-lived, accomplishment. But from behind the placid facade, one scandal after another erupted into the open. The most spectacular was the Teapot Dome affair, in which Secretary of the Interior Albert B. Fall and Secretary of the Navy Edwin Denby were accused of giving oilmen Edward Doheny and Harry Sinclair access to valuable oil reserves set aside for the navy. In 1922, Doheny leased the Elk Hills reserve in California and Sinclair leased the Teapot Dome reserve in Wyoming. In return, the federal government received only some oil-storage tanks in Hawaii. A Senate investigation showed that Doheny had loaned $100,000 to Fall in 1921 without interest or collateral, and that after Fall had resigned from

the cabinet in 1923, Sinclair had "loaned" him $250,000. Fall was convicted of bribery and sentenced to serve one year in prison and to pay a $100,000 fine. The Supreme Court declared the oil leases invalid in 1927.

Harding himself was personally honest, but that was more than could be said for some of his friends. The Veterans Bureau scandal was one example of the President's naive trust in people. On a visit to Hawaii he met and was impressed by one Charles R. Forbes, a jovial go-getter whose chief distinction was his courageous war record—although, oddly enough, it turned out that he had once been an army deserter. In 1921, Harding appointed his newfound friend custodian of veterans' affairs. During the two years Forbes held the office, $200,000,000 went astray. Contracts for hospital construction were let without regard to low bidders, and "surplus" goods were sold at unbelievably low prices, after which similar items were bought at the going market rate. In 1926, Forbes was sentenced to the federal penitentiary for two years and fined $10,000.

Another Harding appointee, Alien Property Custodian Thomas W. Miller, and a member of the Ohio gang named Jesse Smith made $100,000 in a transaction involving the return of the American Metal Company to its former German owners. Part of the money went to Attorney General Harry Daugherty. Miller went to prison for fraud; Smith committed suicide. When Daugherty refused to testify before a Senate investigating committee, Harding's successor, Coolidge, dismissed him.

Most of the scandals broke after Harding's death on August 2, 1923, midway through his term. Montana's two Senators, Thomas J. Walsh and Burton K. Wheeler, exposed the Teapot Dome giveaway and investigated irregularities in the Justice Department. Harding himself perhaps best explained his difficulties when he told journalist William Allen White, "I have no trouble with my enemies. . . . But my damned friends—they're the ones that keep me walking the floor nights!"

Calvin the Cool

When Calvin Coolidge succeeded Harding, America had a President who was as different from his predecessor as any man could be. The quiet New Englander had been almost unnoticed as Vice-President. Summarizing his meager duties, William Allen White wrote, "So Coolidge, silently dining and meekly clowning his quiet way through official Washington society by night and watching the Senate by day with no responsibilities, no anxieties, except to send a part of his pay check every month back to his Northampton bank to watch the $25,000 grow and grow—symbolizing the doctrine, work and save—he was, as it were, politically embalmed."

As President, Coolidge was in many ways a stranger to the Roaring Twen-

ties. It had been many years since Americans had seen a farm boy enter the White House, and now, in this new age of mechanization and urbanization, Coolidge seemed somehow a relic of the vanished past. But it did not take the businessman long to discover that in certain respects the new President was in tune with the times: His conservatism, his thorough advocacy of *laissez faire*, and his admiration of the masters of capital soon made him a favorite of the business community.

When the Republicans met at Cleveland in 1924, the convention was well organized for Coolidge and he was easily nominated. The Democratic candidate, John W. Davis, was a wealthy corporation lawyer. That year the Progressive Party made its final bid for the Presidency, nominating Robert LaFollette of Wisconsin and Burton K. Wheeler. LaFollette did get his own state's 13 electoral votes, but the nation was not seriously tempted to elect a reform candidate at a time of unbounded prosperity. In spite of the scandals of the Harding administration, voters followed the injunction of Republican Party leaders to "Keep cool with Coolidge" and returned the prim, silent "Cal" to office by a majority of 382 to 136 electoral votes.

Late in the summer of 1927, Calvin Coolidge went fishing in the Black Hills of South Dakota. Reporters had come along on the off-chance that "Silent Cal" might say something of

In May, 1932, the magazine Vanity Fair *was still spoofing Coolidge's well-known taciturnity by pairing him with Greta Garbo in its series of "impossible interviews."*

interest. He did. One day he crisply announced, "I do not choose to run for President in 1928." That was all.

This surprising decision produced the usual crop of favorite sons and other prospective candidates, but Herbert Hoover, well known to Americans for his brilliant record in war relief and his capable performance as a cabinet member under both Hard-

1125

ing and Coolidge, was easily the strongest. When the Republicans convened at Kansas City in June, 1928, the Secretary of Commerce was duly nominated.

Meanwhile, the Democrats passed up popular Governor Albert C. Ritchie of Maryland, and Montana's Senator Thomas J. Walsh of Teapot Dome fame, in favor of New York's flamboyant Governor Alfred E. Smith. A product of the slums of Manhattan's Lower East Side, the "Happy Warrior" (as Franklin D. Roosevelt called him), was chosen on the first ballot. But once again Democratic prospects were poor, for Smith, who was both

© 1934 CONDE NAST PUBLICATIONS

The exuberance of Al Smith, the Irishman from the slums of New York who ran for President, is caught in this caricature.

wet and a Catholic, faced an uphill fight in a nation that was both dry and predominantly Protestant.

"Sweep the country with Hoover"

In the contest that followed, issues were largely evaded. A vicious whispering campaign made it appear that Smith's bad grammar and the threat of Papal interference at the White House were equally great dangers to the nation's future. Virtually overlooked as an issue was the facade of paper prosperity behind which there were urgent problems that demanded solution (ominously enough, just two days before Hoover was nominated, the stock market suffered a brief and near-disastrous crash). Hoover and his running mate, Senator Charles Curtis, said little about such matters, but their silence seemed to have its reward: They won by 444 to 87 electoral votes—the third Republican landslide in a row. As the Democrats discovered to their chagrin, prosperity was unbeatable at the polls.

When Hoover took office in March, 1929, the country welcomed him as the ideal successor to Coolidge. He objected to any government interference in business affairs on the ground that it was detrimental not only to economic life but to liberty itself. As he said during the campaign, "Economic freedom cannot be sacrificed if political freedom is to be preserved." In 1929, these were the words that perfectly matched the mood of the nation. Few could foresee that America was on the verge of the worst depression in its history.

In retrospect, the roaring aspect of the Roaring Twenties seems like a gaudy false front for a structure that was beginning to show signs of an alarming deterioration from within. Behind the bright exterior, serious stresses and strains could be detected, and although a variety of remedies were tried, most would prove tragically shortsighted.

For example, the tariff issue had not lost any of its perplexities, and its ramifications went much farther than simply offering protection to American farms and factories. At a time when isolationism and a desire for economic self-sufficiency prevailed, high-tariff proponents had little difficulty in persuading Congress to pass the Fordney-McCumber Tariff of 1922, which contained the highest rates in the nation's history. The result was disastrous. International trade, which had been growing steadily since the war's end, was checked, and other nations adopted retaliatory tariffs, causing American exports to diminish even more. Even more prohibitive was the Smoot-Hawley Tariff of 1930. At Hoover's suggestion, tariff makers were set to work in an attempt to protect the American farmer from foreign competition. Before they were through, a thousand tariff increases were suggested, all but 75 of which were for industry, not agriculture. Within two years, 25 countries had retaliated, raising their own tariffs.

On Inauguration Day, 1929, Coolidge, looking more solemn than usual, stands next to President-elect Herbert Hoover.

Instead of gaining the needed trade, Americans watched their exports continue to fall off. As far as commerce was concerned, this act of "splendid isolation" merely deepened the depression then under way.

Transportation was another economic problem of the '20s. America's merchant marine, for example, found itself in increasingly serious difficulties. During the war, it had been controlled by the government, but when peace came, there was a great demand to return it to private hands. As a result of the Merchant Marine Act of

1127

1920, ships were sold to individuals and to shipping companies on most reasonable terms. Moreover, preferential rates were given to goods and persons carried to the United States from foreign countries in American ships. And subsidies of from $30,000,000 to $50,000,000 a year were paid to companies whose income was not great enough to meet their cost of operation. The act even went so far as to restrict trade with American colonial possessions to American ships —a mercantilist policy that seemed almost a throwback to the 18th century. Yet for all these inducements, the business done by American shipping lines declined steadily during the decade. High wages, high construction costs, and high operating expenses were blamed for the nation's inability to compete with foreign shipping companies. The postwar years also saw a changed policy toward the railroads. Wilson had set the tone in his annual message to Congress in December, 1918, when he criticized a course of "restraint without development."

The Transportation Act of 1920 returned the roads to private ownership, and at the same time laid down rules for a new kind of control. Although the Interstate Commerce Commission was empowered to govern rates, the railroads were assured a return on their investment of at least 5 1/2%. A "recapture clause" provided that one-half of all earnings above 6% should be turned over to the government and put in a revolving fund for the benefit of the weaker roads. Instead of "trust busting," the act took a long step toward consolidation under government sponsorship—a step that fell just short of nationalization.

A much newer industry, which presented problems of its own, was electric power. By 1920, the majority of American homes had electricity, and with the abundance of new electrical appliances on the market, the industry mushroomed. That year a Federal Power Commission came into existence. Although it was authorized to issue licenses for the construction and operation of facilities for the development of electric power, experience showed that it had little ability to control rates or services. Nor was it able to regulate the growth and spread of huge power monopolies. As local companies merged into larger organizations, they in turn became components of huge holding companies. By 1920, about 12 of these systems controlled more than 75% of the power generated in the nation. One man, Samuel Insull of Chicago, pyramided his holding and investment companies until he had interests in nearly 4,800 communities in 30 different states. Insull was chairman of the board of 65 different companies and the president of 11 others. But as time went on, he overextended himself. His stocks were heavily watered, and when the crash came in 1929, the dam burst. His empire gone, Insull fled the country; he died leaving $1,000 in cash and debts of $14,000,000. It

The merchant ships that were built by the government during the war, in ship-yards like this one painted by Jonas Lie, were afterward sold to private companies.

was disasters of that kind that would later help to convince the public that greater federal control and even federally built and operated power projects were in its best interests.

The business of farming

By the 1920s the American farmer had become something of a businessman himself. The age-old figure of the honest plowman following the endless single furrow had given way to that of an agricultural technician operating expensive gasoline-driven machinery; the day of the small farmer was rapidly passing. Now powerful tractors pulled multiple plows in the springtime and complicated, costly wheat combines in the fall.

When the decade began, the prospects for American agriculture had seemed bright. Wartime prices had been high—artificially high. But in the next few years, American markets in Europe dwindled as that battered continent recovered from the effects of the war and was once more able to feed its own population. To compli-

1129

cate matters, farms had to face an increasingly fierce competition in the export of such basic commodities as grain from countries like Russia, Canada, Australia, and Argentina. The price of agricultural goods, sold on a world market, sank steadily. In an attempt to counter the ill effects of this decline, American farmers tried to cut their losses by growing bigger crops. But prices merely continued to plummet, and as the costs of the machinery necessary for large-scale operations multiplied, the farmer found himself ever more deeply in debt.

Legislative attempts to help agriculture were older than the national government itself. From the time of the Ordinance of 1785, under the Articles of Confederation, lawmakers had tried to aid Americans who lived off the soil. In 1921, Congress tried once more, this time raising the tariff duties on foreign agricultural products. As the United States exported more foodstuffs than it imported, the maneuver accomplished little or nothing. The farm bloc in Congress also pushed through the Packers and Stockyards Act (1921) in an attempt to break up packing-company monopolies that were accused of taking too large a profit. The Grain Futures Trading Act was similarly designed to put a stop to monopolies and price manipulations in the grain market. The Capper-Volstead Cooperative Marketing Act (1922) attempted to protect small farmers who had grouped together in cooperatives by

exempting them from prosecution under the Sherman Antitrust Act.

More tangible help came in the form of loans. In 1921, Congress enlarged the powers of the War Finance Corporation by allowing it to extend aid to farmers. The Federal Intermediate Credit Act of 1923 set up 12 regional banks and provided each institution with $5,000,000. By 1930, farmers had borrowed a total of $3,000,000,000 from the various sources available to them.

Such efforts were helpful, but they were essentially no more than stopgap measures. During the whole decade of the '20s, the one attempt to get to the root of the farm problem was the McNary-Haugen Farm Relief Bill. It provided for a federal farm board to fix the local price of grain and buy the surplus. This would either be stored until the price rose or sold abroad at the going world-market price. To compensate for the loss if the federal farm board had to sell outside the country, the bill proposed that the government levy an "equalization fee" against grain sold on the domestic market. Twice the act passed Congress and twice Coolidge vetoed it, for he believed it included a price-fixing principal and also benefited special groups and was therefore unconstitutional.

More successful was the Agricultural Marketing Bill, passed in 1929 and signed by Hoover. It established an eight-member Federal Farm Board, headed by the Secretary of Agriculture, to encourage the development of agricultural cooperatives and to make loans to them. The board tried to buy up surplus wheat and managed, in 1931, to raise the price 20¢ to 30¢ above the going rate on the world market. It did the same with cotton. But when surpluses became too great to buy up, the program collapsed, and agricultural prices fell to new lows. Hoover discovered, as would his successors, that merely buying surpluses would not and could not solve the problem of overproduction.

The plight of the worker

The farmer was not the only one who stood back and enviously watched the businessman enjoy the biggest boom in the nation's history, for the industrial worker, too, did not always share in the general prosperity. Many people believed that labor had significantly bettered its lot during the war, but its gains were largely superficial. It is true that during 1914–18 the major union organization—the American Federation of Labor—had doubled its strength. In 1920, it stood at the peak of its power, with 4,000,000 members. Within a decade, however, membership had fallen by over 1,000,000. One reason was the apathy of the labor movement itself; another was the prevailing conservatism of the period, which regarded organized labor as a threat to continued prosperity.

Organized labor did little to combat the adverse trend. When Samuel Gompers died in 1924 and William Green took over the A.F.L., the organization seemed to become a dig-

By 1920, the days of the small farmer were numbered, and powerful tractors like the one above were making possible the development of large farm operations.

Millworker John Kane painted Turtle Creek Valley's steelworks in Pennsylvania in 1922, when a recession had set in and organized labor was losing ground.

nified, conservative, and even timid satellite of big business, retaining few of its old crusading instincts. Corporations followed a policy of "killing with kindness" any segments of labor that threatened to be aggressive. Workers were encouraged, through the distribution of various benefits, to join company-sponsored unions. By mid-decade there were more than 400 of these organizations, with their total membership half that of those affiliated with the A.F.L. But the leadership of the A.F.L. seemed uninclined to fight back. It quietly accepted the rise of the company unions, making no real attempt to remain independ-

ent of what has been called welfare capitalism.

Nor was the businessman's government taking any chances on a labor resurgence. The hostility of the courts rivaled that of the 1890s. In *Hammer vs. Dagenhart* (1918) and *Bailey vs. Drexel Furniture Company* (1922), the Supreme Court quashed the efforts of Congress to end child labor. Also, there was a growing use of the injunction in labor disputes. The Supreme Court struck hard at labor in *Coppage vs. Kansas* (1915) when it upheld the yellow-dog contract—one that forbids employees to join a union. In *Adkins vs. Children's Hospital*

When Thomas Hart Benton painted his oil-rich Boom Town *in 1928, the Harding administration's oil scandals were still before the public and the courts.*

(1923) the court ruled, in effect, that minimum wage laws were unconstitutional. Labor still had the right to boycott, strike, and picket despite these decisions, but the laws were made so restrictive that even these traditional weapons were badly weakened.

The isolationist impulse

A part of the prevailing political conservatism of the '20s was isolationism. There seemed to be a desire to retreat within America's ramparts and let the rest of the world take care of its own problems. During the early part of Harding's administration, communications from the League of Nations were not even answered, and the government refused, in reality, to recognize its existence. Throughout the '20s and '30s, the United States declined membership in the World Court, even though every President from Harding to Franklin D. Roosevelt recommended participation. Each attempt to join was blocked by the Senate, either by outright rejection or by the inclusion of reservations that member nations would not accept.

The main exception to this lone-wolf policy was the Washington Conference in 1921. America emerged from the war as the world's leading

1133

economic power; if its wartime program of armament had been continued, she would have become the dominant military and naval power as well.

In August, 1921, Secretary of State Charles Evans Hughes invited all major powers except Russia to a conference on the limitation of armaments. There was a willing response; Great Britain in particular had little desire to maintain a huge military establishment that had to be financed by exorbitant taxes. The purpose of the conference was twofold: One was to consider naval disarmament, and the other was to discuss ways of easing tensions in the Pacific and the Far East, where the Western nations felt their colonial interests were being threatened by the rapid and increasingly militant expansion of the Japanese Empire. Representatives from the United States, Great Britain, France, Italy, and Japan, as well as those from such minor powers as China, Belgium, the Netherlands, and Portugal attended. Meeting at Washington for the first time on November 12, the diplomats negotiated until February 6, 1922. Their work is most often remembered for the naval disarmament treaty, one of nine it produced. In this treaty, the United States, Great Britain, and Japan agreed to a limitation of the number of battleships in their fleets. The first two were to be allowed 500,000 tons each, Japan was to have 300,000 tons —or a ratio of 5-5-3. To their disappointment, France and Italy were obliged to settle for 175,000 tons each.

Two of the other treaties dealt with the Far Eastern problem. In one involving the United States, Great Britain, France, and Japan, the signers agreed to respect the rights of one another in the Pacific and to refer all major disputes to arbitration. A nine-power treaty, signed by the "Big Five" as well as Holland, Portugal, China, and Belgium, pledged the territorial integrity of China and reaffirmed the open-door principle.

Later, in 1927, President Coolidge called for the five great powers to meet at Geneva to consider limitations on ships not covered by the naval disarmament treaty. France and Italy refused to attend, and the United States, Britain, and Japan could not agree upon a formula. The failure put a strain on Anglo-American relations and foreshadowed Japan's later unwillingness to abide by the earlier agreement.

A final gesture toward permanent world peace was the Kellogg-Briand Pact of 1928, put forward by the United States and France. This idealistic document, which attempted to "outlaw" war "as an instrument of national policy," was approved by 15 nations (62 eventually signed it). Although widely popular, it was to prove ineffectual; as Senator James A. Reed of Missouri said, it was little more than an "international kiss." Events of the next decade would bear tragic witness that war could not be abolished by the flourish of a pen.

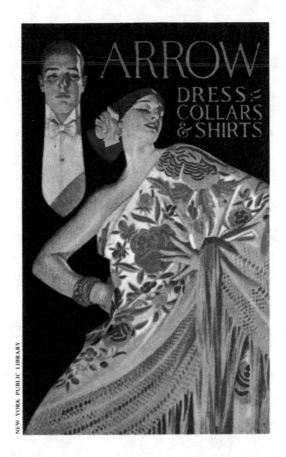

NEW YORK PUBLIC LIBRARY

AMERICA AS ADVERTISED

From World War I through the '20s, advertising reflected the opulence and the ta-
boos of the times. The Arrow collar (above) spread its full-dress wings. The better
automobiles abandoned dependability as their chief sales theme and became status
symbols. Bathroom fixtures were not yet seen in full, but peeked at through cur-
tains of Oriental richness. The home heater was for the living room, just as the
pipe organ was. Girls did not smoke in advertisements—only encouraged their
men to do so. Jell-O was pictured, by Maxfield Parrish, as fit for king and queen.
Cosmetics and women's shoes and hosiery were presented by *femmes fatales*,
but corsets, underwear, and swimming suits were offered with no help from allur-
ing female figures. As for the men's-wear models, Mother Nature would not have
recognized them. These old advertisements speak for themselves, without captions.

1135

PIERCE-ARROW

No words do justice to the fine feeling that the new PIERCE-ARROW gives—the fine feeling of power ample and unfailing, so perfectly applied that the car increases its service and comfort with nothing to detract from them.

THE PIERCE ARROW MOTOR CAR COMPANY · BUFFALO, NEW YOR

Chrysler Imperial Convertible Coupe (wire wheels extra), $1995

IMPERIAL

THE new Chrysler Imperial is a car intended essentially for the connoisseurs among motorists—that exclusive circle whose discrimination is satisfied with nothing short of the best in Chrysler power, smoothness, fineness and beauty. ¶ The distinguished characteristics of the Chrysler Imperial reveal the latest and utmost ingenuity of Chrysler styling, engineering and craftsmanship. ¶ Every motorist who appreciates a car of true custom quality will find in the new Imperial a type of beauty and behavior unlike and beyond anything heretofore known in the field of the very finest.

Roadster $2675; Sedan (5-passenger), $2975; Town Sedan, $2975; Standard Coupe, $2995; Convertible Coupe, $2995; Phaeton (7-passenger), $3095; Sedan (7-passenger), $3095; Sedan-Limousine, $3475; Custom-built Phaeton (4-passenger), $3855. All prices f. o. b. factory.

PHAETON Four-Passenger

COLE

Eight Ninety

It has been the privilege of the producers of the Cole to incorporate in its building those features that mark it as

truly

A FINER CAR

COLE MOTOR CAR COMPANY
INDIANAPOLIS, U. S. A.

There's a Touch of Tomorrow in All Cole Ones Today

LINCOLN

Seven Passenger Sedan

The distinguished Lincoln clientele includes many who prefer the popular Sedan body type so admirably adapted to family use. They are content with no less than Lincoln well-balanced excellence, luxurious appointments, body beauty and obedient, effortless performance. The magnificent Seven-Passenger Sedan is designed for these Lincoln patrons.

LINCOLN MOTOR COMPANY
Division of Ford Motor Company

A Charming Something with lithe and youthful lines —
a thoroughbred descendant of a roving race —inspired with the verve of modern youth —and dressed up like nobody's business —in short ready to go somewhere —and going. That's the new Jordan Playboy.

"Standard"
PLUMBING FIXTURES

Standard Sanitary Mfg. Co.
Pittsburgh

The Magic Rug of the Twentieth Century

"Magic" It's cleaned with a few whisks of a dry mop.
"Magic" It's made on a felt base with an enamel-like surface in a score of patterns and colors.

"Magic" It's made absolutely waterproof to insure long wear.
"Magic" It's sold at retail in many sizes from 3½ to 5⅓ by, a ton of continuous production.

If every woman knew what every present owner knows, every home would have a Bird's Neponset Rug. If any salesman say "It's Bird's" that's really all you need to know. Look for the patented red seal on back.

NEW YORK   CHICAGO   DALLAS
PHILADELPHIA   DETROIT   KANSAS CITY
ATLANTA   ST. PAUL   SEATTLE
SAN FRANCISCO   LOS ANGELES

BIRD & SON, Inc.
Established 1795
Factories in Felt-Base Floor Coverings,
EAST WALPOLE, MASS.

Manufacturers of Bird's Twin Shingles,
Bird's Paroid Roofings, Bird's Neponset Black Building Paper
and Bird's Wall Board

Bird's [BIRD NEPONSET PRODUCTS] Rugs
DEFY WATER AND WEAR

THE ESTEY RESIDENCE PIPE ORGAN

ONE THRILLS at the very idea of a pipe organ in the home. It is such a majestic instrument. It adds so much to the dignity, the unusualness of even the most complete and modern house. Its music is so satisfying. It appeals to all.

And a pipe organ is so easily attainable. We have solved all the problems. We are able to build an organ to fit any house, and at almost any price. The Estey Residence Organ can be played auto-matically by The Estey Organist, so that skill and training are unnecessary. But this does not interfere with its being a perfect instrument for the human player.

THE ESTEY ORGAN COMPANY, *Brattleboro, Vermont*

Studios in NEW YORK, 11 West 49th Street
CHICAGO, Lyon & Healy
PHILADELPHIA, 1701 Walnut Street
BOSTON, 120 Boylston Street
LOS ANGELES, 653 South Hill Street

© A. R. Coy, 1926

A Welcome Addition to Any Home

LIKE the new arrival, ARCOLA is a most welcome and important addition, changing the house into a home, to benefit and gladden the entire family! In the days of creeping childhood and growing youth, there is greatest need to guard with reliable, protecting ARCOLA warmth, all floors, nooks and corners. Ideal ARCOLA Hot Water Heating will make the whole house a healthful playground—and a delightful relaxing place, as well, for grown-ups and the elderly.

ARCOLA keeps the rooms at 72°, all through—or at any other degree you set—regardless of weather changes. The Automatic Controller watches the fire, saving enough fuel in five years to repay cost of the ARCOLA. For the rest of your life you have a big interest-earning investment—the cleanliest, health-giving warmth for baby and all! Examine all the ARCOLA features at any heating and plumbing store. Note its handsome porcelain-enameled jacket. Burns ANY fuel. New low price due to great volume of sales.

ARCOLA
(T. M. Reg. U.S. Pat. Off.)
Hot Water Radiator Heat

Gives you the comfort you have always wanted! Enjoy an ARCOLA at once, and pay in ten months! If you have a small home, bungalow, single flat, store, shop, office, etc., write us, Dept. 1, 1807 Elmwood Ave., Buffalo, for (free) book on ARCOLA—full of valuable heating information. Make this fine addition to your home today!

AMERICAN RADIATOR COMPANY

Showrooms and sales offices: New York, Boston, Providence, Philadelphia, Baltimore, Washington, Buffalo, Pittsburgh, Cleveland, Detroit, Cincinnati, Atlanta, Chicago, Milwaukee, Indianapolis, St. Louis, St. Paul, Omaha, Kansas City, Denver, San Francisco, Los Angeles, Seattle
Toronto, London, Paris, Milan, Brussels, Berlin

Makers of IDEAL BOILERS

For larger buildings: Type "A" Machine, Arco, Water Tube, Soft Coal Smokeless; factory heating boilers and other heating, ventilating and cooling products

January 1926 Good Housekeeping

Florient
Flowers of the Orient

AN added charm of Florient Talc is the color of the powder. This is most unusual and distinctive—just off the white. The rare Oriental fragrance and delicate fineness of the powder itself also explain the popularity of Colgate's Florient—the new superfine Talc.

Florient, you will remember, gained first place in an International Perfume Contest. As the pure delight of its fragrance won favor—so will the grace and beauty of the new box in which Florient Talc comes to you.

An attractive miniature box of Florient Talc will be sent upon request if you mention *Vogue*.

COLGATE & CO.   *Est. 1806*   **New York**

The exquisite fragrance of Florient is now embodied also in Extract Toilet Water, in Face Powder, and in Soap.

LILY OF FRANCE CORSET

THE LILY OF FRANCE IS A BEAUTIFUL
CORSET WORN BY BEAUTIFUL WOMEN
TO MAKE THEM MORE BEAUTIFUL.

SEND FOR FREE
DE LUXE
STYLE CATALOGUE   LILY OF FRANCE CORSET CO. 303 SIXTH AVE, NEW YORK

McCallum SILK HOSIERY

"You just know she wears them"

WHEN you wear McCallum Silk Stockings
there comes that little extra thrill of wearing the
recognized best.

Nowhere will you find as many styles and
designs in silk stockings as you will
find in McCallum. There are plain
ones for every-day wear, clocked
models for sports wear, exquisite
sheer ones for formal occasions.

Among the most popular numbers are 105—
113—122—199 in black, and 152—153—199 in
colors. A copy of our illustrated catalogue showing a great many McCallum models will be sent
to you free upon request.

Every shop does not carry
McCallum Silk Stockings, but
those that have the loveliest
things do.

McCallum
Silk Hosiery

CAMMEYER
Brands De Luxe
677-Fifth Avenue
New York

Exclusive Footwear for Women

WOMEN are learning that
the secret of appearing
smartly turned-out on the beach
lies in the selection of one of
the new Tom Wye Swimming
Suits. They can be had in
two-piece or California style
garments made of our specially
knit material, in all the season's
most wanted shades.

We will gladly send you the
name of the nearest merchant
who can supply you.

TOM WYE, Inc., *Winchendon, Mass.*

1142

Women to whom smartness of design is as important as dainty luxury of fabric highly prize "Niagara Maid" UNDERWEAR of silk

DISTINCTION in style, combined with simplicity, is not easy to attain. Real art in designing and skill in tailoring make this combination possible. A slant pocket style, universally liked.

THE WAYNE

DEPEND ON KUPPENHEIMER VALUE

Kuppenheimer merchants are now showing suits of TIGERTWIST, TROJAN WEAVE and CASTILIANS - original in pattern and color - the ranking fabrics from the world's looms. Created to give you fine style and extra value - just as FAMOUS FIFTIES set the $50 standard.

Fur Collar Coat. There comes a time when a man owes himself a fur collar over-garment. The Kuppenheimer form-fitting overcoat with Hudson Seal collar, or the Blizzard Ulster with broad Beaver collar, is unquestionably good form for street wear, dress or motoring.

CLOTHES APPEARANCE IS important to your success—don't slight it—he judged by your clothes taste, Kuppenheimer good clothes.

You'll not only buy the best made clothes, but you'll buy the best clothes appearance. You never go wrong, any way, selecting Kuppenheimer clothes.

The popular Double Breasted at its best—
in Hickey-Freeman Customized Clothes.

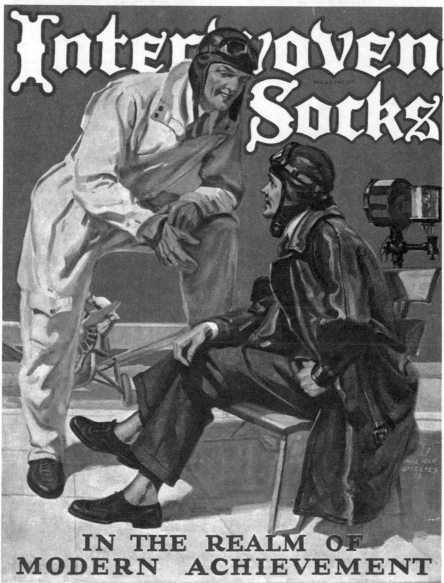

IN THE REALM OF
MODERN ACHIEVEMENT

JUDGE

1146

CHAPTER 39

THE ROARING TWENTIES

Hardly had the Roaring Twenties ended when that flamboyant decade began to take on the aura of legend. Although the revolution in morals was its most sensational manifestation, other forces contributed equally to its special quality.

It was, for one thing, an age of unabashed materialism. Enormous paper profits were made not only by the large stock speculators but by the smallest investors; "playing the market" became a national pastime. By putting up a nominal sum, one could "buy on margin"—that is, hold stocks for only a small percentage of their total value. Thus the mechanic, the storekeeper, the salesman, and anyone else in the middle-income groups could participate with the dream of parlaying his down payment into big money. The extent to which the "little people" played the market encouraged

The flapper, with lipstick and rolled stockings, and the callow collegian, with hip flask, cigarette holder, and flashy roadster, were stock characters in the gallery of John Held, Jr., portraitist of the Jazz Age. Here they gaily greet the New Year of 1925 from the cover of Judge, *a humor magazine of the day.*

the formation of huge industrial and commercial empires, some of which, unfortunately, were supported by watered stock. When the market broke late in 1929, the whole structure tumbled like a house of cards. Instead of wiping out only a comparatively few professional gamblers, the crash ruined thousands of amateur "investors," many of whom had mortgaged everything they owned.

But as the market spiraled ever upward, and the boom continued unabated, few concerned themselves with any unhappy thoughts that the worst might happen. The easy-come, easy-go philosophy induced millions to fill their homes with every convenience available, and in answer to the demand, manufacturers turned out a mounting volume of radios, refrigerators, irons, toasters, vacuum cleaners, and washing machines. Everyone had to have an automobile—and better, two. To encourage sales, dealers began to make goods available "on time." Like the speculator who could buy his stock for a small amount down, the buyer of automobiles and home appliances had only to make a token payment to take his new acquisition out of the showroom. Now millions of Americans actually owned only 10% to 20% of each item they contracted for, and in this sense they, too, were buying on margin.

Enormous sums of money were also spent on entertainment—and in the 1920s there was no dearth of amusements. The jazz band with its wild, syncopated rhythms became as much a symbol of the era as the stock market, and in sedate ballrooms and speakeasies, in college fraternity houses and country clubs, millions danced to the rage of the moment—the fox trot, the lame duck, the grizzly bear, the black bottom, or, most famous of all, the Charleston. In the big cities, more lavish entertainment could be found in the theater "spectacles" staged by such enterprising showmen as Florenz Ziegfeld and Earl Carroll, who found it hugely profitable to "glorify" the American girl.

Of all popular art forms, however, the movies captured the fancy of the public most vividly. Not only were they still a novelty, but Hollywood producers had managed to gauge with

In the '20s, female hearts raced madly over Rudolph Valentino, an Italian immigrant gardener whom chance had made into a Great Lover in the guise of an actor.

remarkable success the tempo of the times. Americans wanted something daring and bizarre, and that is what they got. One purveyor of celluloid excitement advertised his product with typical flamboyance: "Brilliant men, beautiful jazz babies, champagne baths, midnight revels, petting parties in the purple dawn." Rivals offered such enticements as *Sinners in Silk* and *Women Who Give*.

Sex appeal was the big drawing card. To the public, acting talent seemed to mean little (and it was hard to discern anyway, as the "talkies," which demanded something more than emotional overplaying, were not introduced until late in the decade). The leading cinematic sex symbol was Rudolph Valentino, an Italian immigrant gardener who could offer his public little more than long sideburns and a passionate Latin manner. Yet he was catapulted to international fame as a Great Lover in such vehicles as *The Sheik* and *The Four Horsemen of the Apocalypse*. He obviously heightened the heartbeat of women of all ages, for when he died in 1926, some 30,000 fans crowded around the New York mortician's where he lay in state, and a near-riot took place as they jostled one another for one last look. Before his body could be interred, Tin Pan Alley capitalized upon the event by turning out *There's a New Star in Heaven Tonight,* with Valentino on the sheet-music cover.

Sports competed with movies for public attention, and athletes, too, be-

Babe Ruth, once a pitcher, became a great box-office attraction after he started hitting home runs for the Yankees. He was already a legend, two years before retirement, when he appeared on Vanity Fair.

came national idols. An Illinois youngster named Harold "Red" Grange brought college football to the fore with his Saturday afternoon touchdown rampages. When he quit school to join the professional Chicago Bears, he became such a drawing card that he received a salary which, one writer estimated, amounted to $1,000 for every

George Bellows painted Argentina's Luis Firpo, "Wild Bull of the Pampas,"
knocking Jack Dempsey out of the ring in 1923, but Dempsey came back to win.

minute he spent on the football field.

The rough-and-tumble of the grid-iron was closely rivaled by the violent action of the boxing ring. Here William Harrison "Jack" Dempsey was the undisputed king until 1926, when a former marine, Gene Tunney, uncrowned him one rainy September night in Philadelphia. The return bout, held in Chicago, attracted over 100,000 fight fans, who paid more than $2,500,000 to see Dempsey's unsuccessful comeback attempt. Millions more flocked to baseball parks, where a truly American game had be-come a big business. Here reigned George Herman "Babe" Ruth, the "Sultan of Swat," whose powerful swing netted him a record-breaking 60 home runs in one season (1927) and nearly $1,500,000 during his career, as well as another $500,000 from vaudeville appearances, commercial endorsements, and movies.

The "noble experiment"

When the doughboys came back, they found many changes; not the least was an absence of alcoholic beverages. The nation (much of which

1150

was already dry) had decided to abolish the saloon once and for all: Prohibition—the "noble experiment"—had come at last. "The country accepted it," Frederick Lewis Allen wrote, "not only willingly, but almost absent-mindedly." When the Eighteenth Amendment came before the Senate in 1917, it was passed by a one-sided vote after only 13 hours of debate. When the House of Representatives accepted it a few months later, the debate upon the amendment as a whole occupied only a single day. The state legislatures ratified it in short order; by January, 1919, some two months after the armistice, the necessary three-quarters of the states had fallen into line and the amendment was part of the Constitution. Officially, nationwide prohibition was supposed to take effect on January 16, 1920; actually, under the Wartime Prohibition Law, passed just before the armistice, it began in the summer of 1919.

A majority of Americans probably endorsed prohibition in the beginning, but the public rapidly grew disenchanted with it. The hip flask, filled with illicit, or "bootleg," whiskey and displayed openly and shamelessly, soon became another familiar symbol of the era. Every community of any size had its "speakeasies," where homemade and imported alcoholic beverages could be bought.

The speakeasies did a rushing business. Keeping them supplied was an occupation for many thousands of bootleggers, rumrunners, and beer barons, who were obliged to work beyond the pale of the law. Often their rivalries and differences of opinion resulted in open warfare and gangland slayings. Thanks to wartime technology, they had new and deadly weapons at their disposal—hand grenades (suitable for blowing up com-

A typical New York speakeasy entrance was under the stoop of a brownstone. The customers had to pass scrutiny to get in.

1151

petitors' establishments), submachine guns, and fast boats and getaway cars.

The Eighteenth Amendment had a host of both defenders and detractors. The drys insisted it was a success, sharply reducing deaths, divorces, accidents, and poverty. But the wets held it was as senseless as the attempts to enforce it were futile. As one notorious figure of the era said, "They might as well have been trying to dry up the Atlantic with a post-office blotter." Franklin P. Adams, in his column in the New York *World,* expressed a similar view:

> *Prohibition is an awful flop.*
>   *We like it.*
> *It can't stop what it's meant to stop.*
>   *We like it.*
> *It's left a trail of graft and slime.*
> *It's filled our land with vice and crime,*
> *It can't prohibit worth a dime.*
>   *Nevertheless, we're for it.*

In other words, those who wanted prohibition could say they had it; those who wanted to drink, drank. Thus, as a social experiment, prohibition proved an utter failure. Not only was it impossible to enforce, but in providing the underworld with its chief source of revenue, it fostered an evil far worse than the one it attempted to suppress. The American public, which had once willingly or at least resignedly accepted prohibition, gradually came to look upon it as the ill-advised measure it was. And yet, because the issue was considered political dynamite, the movement to abol-

ish prohibition made little headway during the '20s. Not until 1933, the first year of Franklin D. Roosevelt's administration, was it repealed.

"100% American"

The war years sharply stimulated American nationalism—a development that became more noticeable as the '20s wore on. It was part of a general pattern of suspicion and retreat that encouraged both commercial and domestic isolation, emphasized home-grown ideas and products, and blurred, if not blinded, the view of events abroad.

For one thing, this national myopia sharply affected immigration policies. Employers who once had welcomed the influx of cheap and docile foreign workers now became frightened by local labor unrest and by what appeared to be the spreading threat of a new and dangerously radical spirit in Europe. Old prejudices against foreigners were sharpened as the practice of blaming labor agitation upon the foreign-born became more common. Ironically, many liberals also joined the mounting clamor, claiming the influx of immigrant

The law sometimes caught up with those who broke it during prohibition. At the top, a shipload of smuggled liquor is seized by revenue agents; in the center, a group is searched for hip flasks; and at the bottom is the aftermath of a raid upon The House of Morgan, a speakeasy owned by top entertainer Helen Morgan.

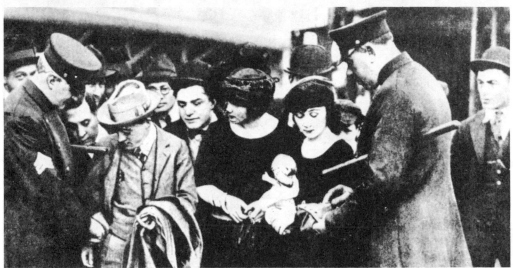

1153

1154

workers was lowering both wages and labor's standard of living. There was a widespread feeling, too, that the newcomers—especially those from southern and eastern Europe—would corrupt not only the American political system but our "racial" stock as well.

Congress responded to these pressures by further tightening immigration laws. Under a law passed in May, 1921, quotas were imposed limiting the number of immigrants in any one year to 3% of the foreign-born of each nationality in the United States in 1910. The law was mainly aimed at immigrants from southern Europe, the bulk of whom had come to America after that year. But it did not cut back the number of new arrivals enough to suit the legislators, who, in 1924, passed an even more restrictive law, reducing the number admitted from 3% to 2% and basing the quota on the census of 1890. This resulted in diminishing the flow of foreign workers to a minute proportion of the American labor force.

Closely allied with antiforeign sentiment was a fear of radical activity, which at times verged on hysteria. In

A prohibition headquarters (top) in New Jersey of a huge liquor syndicate had bulletproof steel walls. The center photograph shows part of what was taken there after a raid. (Note short-wave radio.) At the bottom are victims of Chicago's Valentine's Day massacre, an episode in 1929's ruthless gang wars.

1919, especially, labor unrest was so widespread (in that year alone there were some 3,630 strikes involving over 4,000,000) that many felt a revolution was at hand. The organization of the Communist Party of America did little to ease nervous minds, even though its membership was microscopic. But the so-called "Red scare" rose to a height of frenzy when time bombs addressed to various leaders of business and government were discovered in post offices throughout the land. Only one exploded, blowing off the hands of a Georgia Senator's house servant.

A. Mitchell Palmer, Wilson's Attorney General, thereupon launched an anti-Red campaign that would, before it had run its course, prove the most serious infringement of civil liberties since the Sedition Act of John Adams' day. Although Congress refused to supply the Attorney General with a sedition act of his own, Palmer went ahead, arresting some 6,000 persons in a series of surprise raids on January 2, 1920. His purpose was to round up alien members of the Communist or Communist-Labor Parties, but many of those taken in were American citizens innocent of any connection with communism. The whole procedure was so indiscriminate that in one New England city, those who attempted to visit the imprisoned were jailed on the theory that they, too, must be Communists. After a period of unjustified detention, about one-third of the catch was released; even-

Still disputed are the trial and conviction of Nicola Sacco and Bartolomeo Vanzetti (above) for the murder of a paymaster in 1920. Many thought them innocent.

tually, some 500 aliens were deported.

Meanwhile, the Ku Klux Klan was causing thoughtful Americans concern. Founded during reconstruction, it was revived in the South during the '20s, mainly to guarantee a continuation of white supremacy. Soon, however, it spread across the land and found just as many adherents north of the Mason-Dixon line as south of it. In a catchall program that was anti-Semitic, anti-Catholic, antialien, and, of course, anti-Red, the Klan followed the pattern of its ancestor by putting on nocturnal parades of white-sheeted marchers who intimidated, flogged, and even killed some of those who incurred its displeasure. By the mid-'20s, the membership was reckoned at somewhere between 4,000,000 and 6,000,-000. After a series of lurid scandals involving some of the Klan's leaders, however, the organization fell into a quick decline, and by the end of the decade, the sinister power it once wielded had all but vanished.

Perhaps no event pointed up .the

The '20s saw the rebirth of the bigoted Ku Klux Klan, whose strength was so great for a few years that it could march without interference through Washington.

struggle between political reactionaries and liberals over the Red question more than the Sacco-Vanzetti case. In 1920, two Italian immigrants, Nicola Sacco and Bartolomeo Vanzetti, were arrested as suspects in the murder of a shoe-factory paymaster at South Braintree, Massachusetts. At the trial, in 1921, they were convicted and sentenced to death. To many, the real reason for the verdict was that the men were professed anarchists, immigrants, and pacifists, who had evaded the draft during the war.

There were protests from people of all shades of opinion in the United States, and even in Europe and Latin America there were demonstrations. The trial became an international *cause célèbre.* So great was the uproar that in July, 1927, six years after the trial, Governor Alvan T. Fuller of Massachusetts appointed a commission headed by President Abbott Lawrence Lowell of Harvard to investigate the case. It sustained the verdict, and a month later Sacco and Vanzetti were electrocuted. The out-

Theatre, OCTOBER, 1927

Movie actress Clara Bow became famous only after novelist Elinor Glyn said she had the rare, indefinable quality—"It."

cry of the intellectuals who had spoken for the condemned men reverberated into the next decade, a time of economic turmoil when radical political views did not seem so dangerous.

Culture for the masses

Despite the emphasis upon hip flasks and the ascending hemlines, giddy, pleasure-loving America made some surprising (if sometimes dubious) cultural advances. The transmission of ideas was no longer through the printed word alone, but also through new media produced by the fast growth of technology. The radio, for example, was now available to the average home. By 1921, about $10,000,000 worth of radio sets had been bought; within eight years, annual sales were well over $800,000,000.

By 1928, 10,000,000 receivers were in use. This equaled the figure for all the rest of the world.

Early programs had their limitations, but before long the industry offered a wide range of listening. The day of setting-up exercises early in the morning, followed by recipes and then an extended period of dance music, soon gave way to more varied fare. In 1924, candidates of both political parties used the new medium to disseminate their programs and arguments, and for the first time Americans could sit in on a Presidential campaign.

Movies, of course, competed with radio for the attention of the public. In the more than 20,000 movie houses across the land, some 175,000 miles of film were shown each week to an estimated 100,000,000 customers. In 1927, the motion picture industry realized its dream of supplementing images with sound. When Al Jolson appeared in *The Jazz Singer* and actually sang to the patrons, a revolution took place in the movie world. The "talkie" did not win out over the silent film, however, without serious casualties. To the consternation of some producers, more than one virile hero of the silent screen turned out to have a far from robust voice on the synchronized recording that preceded the sound track.

Despite the growth of radio and the movies, the printed word still continued to command respect. The number of newspapers did decline sharply, but this did not mean fewer readers. More than 2,000 newspapers disappeared between 1914 and 1929, most of them swallowed up by mergers. Magazines, on the other hand, showed large gains, from about 70,000,000 subscribers in 1914 to 111,000,000 in 1925.

A glance at the bookshelf of a home of the '20s—or more particularly the bookshelf of a summer cabin, where a lighter brand of reading was preferred—would have supported the notion that the public was in search of the sensational and bizarre. The predominant theme of many new books seemed to be sex. The trend began at the turn of the decade, when such gifted realistic writers as Sherwood Anderson, John Dos Passos, and Theodore Dreiser chose not to shy away from subjects that hitherto had been forbidden. But soon opportunists appeared who dropped all pretense of art and simply emphasized sex for its own sake. Commenting on the works of Elinor Glyn, a novelist of this period, Mark Sullivan stated, "All her books were utterly worthless, and all were tremendously popular." Mrs. Glyn made one doubtful contribution to the English language when she transformed the simple pronoun "it" into a symbol of sex appeal. Clara Bow, a popular movie star of the day, was publicized as the "It Girl," making millions of her admirers wish that they, too, had "It."

Fortunately, American writers were also concerning themselves with seri-

Al Jolson was a great musical comedy star when he gambled his reputation on the first talking movie, The Jazz Singer.

ous themes, not the least of which was a searching criticism of their own society. In deeply satiric novels like *Main Street* (1920) and *Babbitt* (1922), Sinclair Lewis attacked the smug world of the small-town businessman. Ironically, the Pulitzer Prize committee, in choosing Lewis' *Arrowsmith* (1925), found that it portrayed the "wholesome atmosphere of American life." Few in the Jazz Age seemed offended by the angry author's denunciation of the current moral standards, or the shabbiness of the businessman's motives, or the crass material aspirations of a representative American small town in a boom era.

No single figure personified the times more than F. Scott Fitzgerald. His own life in many ways represented the carefree, hard-drinking,

Chronicler of the Jazz Age, F. Scott Fitzgerald poses lightheartedly with wife Zelda and daughter Frances in Paris in 1925.

Sinclair Lewis—bitter satirist of his country's most revered institutions—is caricatured as throttling the American eagle.

partygoing ideal of many cynical young Americans. Two of his books, *This Side of Paradise* (1920) and *The Beautiful and Damned* (1922), pictured the efforts of the college and young married sets to conceal their sense of insecurity by displays of gaiety. Much better than either of these was *The Great Gatsby* (1925). Although in it Fitzgerald still dealt with the social antics and alcoholism of the gay rich, he tried to probe problems of American life and, in doing so, showed that he had real creative talent.

Cynicism and futility pervaded

other postwar novels. John Dos Passos, a wartime ambulance driver, expressed them in *Three Soldiers* (1921) and *Manhattan Transfer* (1925). In a larger work, the trilogy *U.S.A.,* he presented a panoramic view of America in the '20s that was notable for its bitterness. Ernest Hemingway was another of those who returned home from World War I to write of his generation's disillusion with the Great Crusade. As the hero of his famous war novel *A Farewell to Arms* (1929) put it, "I was embarrassed by the words sacred, glorious, and sacri-

The rugged American was the character Ernest Hemingway portrayed in his novels and assumed for himself in his private life.

John Dos Passos, at 25, wrote Three Soldiers, *his first success, out of the cynicism and futility of his war years.*

fice and the expression in vain. We had heard them, sometimes standing in rain almost out of earshot, so that only the shouted words came through, and had read them, on proclamations, now for a long time, and I had seen nothing sacred, and the things that were glorious had no glory and the sacrifices were like the stockyards in Chicago, if nothing was done with the meat except to bury it . . . Abstract words such as glory, honor, courage, were obscene.''

The "Roaring Twenties," so fondly remembered by later generations, was a strange mixture of calm and conflict. For many, it was the most prosperous time they had ever known, and the ease with which money was made generated an optimism that produced reckless economic thinking and extreme political conservatism. On the other hand, the social behavior of Americans could truly be characterized by the word "revolt." The '20s were 10 years of materialism, ultra-nationalism, isolationism, great prosperity, and declining morality—and yet out of them came a number of the century's significant literary works.

MAIN TEXT CONTINUES IN VOLUME 14

Henry Ford: A Complex Man

A ·SPECIAL CONTRIBUTION BY
ALLAN NEVINS

He built two legends in his lifetime —one about his Model T and another about himself—and he is still one of the most elusive figures in the story of 20th-century America.

One of the most remarkable facts about Henry Ford is that his fame and the Ford legend were born almost simultaneously. He was tossed into international eminence on January 5, 1914, when the Ford Motor Company startled the globe by announcing the incredible minimum wage of $5 a day.

Until then, Henry Ford had touched the national consciousness only glancingly. He had founded the Ford Motor Company in 1903, when already 40; after some years of uncertain struggle, he had produced a model, distinguished from previous Models B, N, and S by the letter T, which precisely filled a ravenous national want; he had erected at Highland Park, just outside Detroit, one of the most efficient factories in the world. He and a group of tireless, gifted associates were developing that implement of global change termed mass production—still little understood (for most people equate it with quantity production, which is merely one of its half-dozen chief components), and then not under-

In this portrait of Henry Ford, painted after he had achieved his success, the lean, eager features suggest his strong emotions and ideas.

stood at all. Ford was, of course, known in the Detroit area as an astonishingly successful manufacturer, but elsewhere until 1914 the name Ford connoted a brand, not a man. Before then, facts on his mind and character are scanty and give no real portrait. But after 1914 the spate of articles, books, and reminiscences becomes torrential. "The Ford and Charlie Chaplin," remarked Will Rogers, "are the best known objects in the world." As the renown grew, unfortunately, so did the confusing legend. As one parodist of the Ford Motor Company slogan put it, "Watch the Ford myths go by!"

Lord Northcliffe, the English publisher, extolled Henry Ford to the British public as a great American. For a time in 1923–24, Ford's quasi-autobiography, translated as *Mein Leben und Werke,* was one of the two best-selling books in Germany. From Sweden to Turkey a new word, *Fordismus,* epitomized the new mass-production engineering, the low-price economy of abundance, and the efficiency speed-up. Throughout Latin America, Ford's personality seemed to sum up American traits. In Russia, painfully aware of her industrial backwardness, Henry Ford was a figure about whom *moujiks* and mechanics dreamed.

In the United States, too, the Ford of fact and the Ford of myth were for a time indistinguishably blended.

Between 1914–29, American masses took Ford to their hearts; every clerk and farmer had his own image of the man. The task of gaining a true portrait was complicated by writers who tried to establish an artificial pat-

FORD MOTOR COMPANY, LONDON

tern, and by Ford himself, who began issuing pronunciamentos and essays in self-portraiture that wove Oriental embroideries about the real man.

At once the most impressive and disturbing fact about Henry Ford is the extent to which he held up a mirror to the modern American character. His technological talents, his feats as an organizer, his individualistic economies, his social blindness, his frequent brilliant insights, his broad veins of ignorance, prejudice, and suspicion at first glance seem unique. But his labyrinthine complications were not different to that degree. For in strength and weakness, pioneering thrust and reactionary conservatism, generosity and self-ishness he came near typifying the America of his time.

What made him a tremendous American force was his clear perception of five fundamental facts—that the American people wanted and needed cars in millions; that a single durable, inexpensive model could meet that demand; that new technological elements (precise standardization of parts, the multi-plication and perfection of machine tools, separation of the job into minutely special-ized functions, quantity manufacture, continu-ous motion, Taylor time studies) could supply the millions of cheap vehicles; that steady price reduction meant steady market expan-sion ("Every time I lower the price a dollar we gain a thousand new buyers"); and that high wages meant high buying power.

All this was obvious, when demonstrated. Until demonstrated, it was so far from patent that the ablest manufacturers scoffed, and Ford had to battle his principal partner and the trend of the times to prove it.

Next to this insight, Henry Ford's most striking gift was his peculiar engineering talent. As a few rare men are born with the power of instantaneously performing intricate mathematical computations, he had the power of divining almost any mechanism at a glance. He *read* engines. Indeed, one associate says that the great engine collections Ford made were his historical library. "They were living things to him, those machines. He could al-

Ford admired Thomas Edison and went with him and tireman Harvey Firestone on camping trips. Left to right: Edison, naturalist John Burroughs, Ford, and Firestone.

On his third attempt at automobile manufacturing, Ford came up with this 1903 Model A runabout. It had two speeds, eight horsepower, and sold for $750.

most diagnose the arrangement by touching it." That gift had been with him when as a boy he took apart and reassembled every watch he could reach, and spent a Sunday afternoon, his father away, in disassembling and restoring much of a steam engine.

Another significant trait was Ford's remarkable capacity for sustained work. The relaxed air that the mature Henry Ford wore in public, together with his well-advertised recreation in square dancing, collecting Americana, and making excursions with Thomas Edison, Harvey Firestone, and John Burroughs, concealed the fact that from boyhood on, he led a singularly laborious, concentrated life. In his prime, his frequent periods of intense industry would have exhausted a less resilient man. At Highland Park and River Rouge his responsibilities were always enormous. But his engineering passion made one important part of them—the responsibility for steady mechanical experiment—almost a refreshment.

Day-to-day study of his activities reveals a man in whose quick brain exploded a steady succession of technological ideas. Writes an associate, "One time he was up at Harbor Beach, where he had a summer cottage, and he was coming home with his son Edsel. Suddenly he said, 'I've got the idea. We're going to put a worm drive on the tractor.'" That idea solved the vexatious problem of power transmission to the rear axle—or so he hoped; and he drove his tractor factory ahead with enhanced zest.

In experimentation, pioneering, the quest of fruitful mechanical innovations, Henry Ford at his apogee was happiest. In 1914–15, he became interested in making a better electric car, and reports spread that he and Edison were collaborating. If the idea proved good (which it did not), he thought of forming a separate company. A later scheme called for the use of plastics in building cars; in fact, a plastic-body car *was* built.

Ford's technological genius was one aspect of a mind peculiar for its intuitive nature. Ford hit upon truths by divination, not ratiocination. His aides credited him with what biographer Dean Marquis termed a "supernormal perceptive faculty." Marquis called him "a dreamer," adding that he had a different view from other men of what was possible and impossible. "I suppose the reason is that men who dream walk by faith, and faith laughs at mountains."

Reliance on intuition partly explains why Ford was so amazingly unpredictable. It also partly explains the crippling isolation of his mind, for a brain that cannot be reasoned with cannot be penetrated. Until 1914, he was open to the counsel of certain men—his partners Alex Malcomson and John S. Gray, his indispensable business manager James Couzens, the brilliant designer Harold Wills, and others. Later, he placed himself beyond advice. His mental isolation "is about as perfect as he can make it," wrote Marquis as early as 1923. His capable production chief, Charles E. Sorensen, who ought to know, believes that Ford had only two lifelong friends—Sorensen himself, and the strong head of his British company, Percival L. D. Perry.

The dreamer, the man of intuitive mind, is usually an artist, and many puzzling contradictions, even many repugnant acts in Ford become comprehensible if we think of him as essentially a man of artistic temperament. His detachment, his arch, wry humor, his constant self-projection into the spotlight, his ability to lift himself above business minutiae, his readiness to do some terrible things with as little seeming consciousness of their quality as Byron or Swift showed in *their* misdeeds—all suggest an artistic bent. The Model T was homely awkwardness itself, but it had artistic elements. Highland Park was the most artistic factory built in America in its day. And what of the aesthetic element in the old dances, old folk songs, old buildings, and old machines Ford loved so well?

Above all, he had the artist's desire to remake the world after his own pattern. His gospel of abundant work, high wages, and low prices; his plans for decentralizing industry to combine it with rural life and rural virtues; his enthusiastic forays into "better"

Ford had a mischievous sense of humor. Here, on an outing, he plays the dour Western badman.

agriculture, education, and recreation were an artist's effort to impose his own vision on life.

There was also a complex enmity between Ford the artist and Ford the untutored countryman whose parents had been Michigan pioneers, and whose own formal education was limited to a few years in a very common school. This conflict twisted the whole skein of his character. An artist needs a cultivated background; Henry Ford's background was that of Anglo-Irish tenant farmers. Though his homely early environment had advantages, its limitations always fettered him.

Henry Ford always remained a countryman in his plain way of living. When his fortune first grew, he said plaintively that the chief difference in his way of life was that "Mrs. Ford no longer does the cooking"—and he preferred her cookery. His puritanic condemnation of smoking, drinking, and marital irregularities conformed to the principles described in Thorstein Veblen's essay *The Country Town*. He was a countryman also in his devotion to work as a virtue in itself. His cure for nearly all ills was more work.

True to the frontiersman's instinct, he preferred trial and error to precise planning. Contemptuous of elaborate record-keeping, he once made a bonfire of forms used to keep track of spare parts. Hostile to meticulous organization, he ran even the huge Highland Park plant without formal titles or administrative grades. He long derided careful cost accounting. In this, thinks one surviving executive, he was right. Success in the automotive industry at first depended not on computation of costs to the third decimal point, but on courageous innovations in design and engineering and on the acceptability of models and prices to the public. Ford stayed in the field of bold experiment; cost accounting might have hampered him.

He also had the frontiersman's intense hatred of monopoly and special privilege. To be sure, he long enjoyed a practical monopoly of the low-priced car, but he could say that he achieved it without favor and without warring on any competitor. His dislike of patents, his course in throwing open to public view and general use Ford machines and methods—all harmonized with the frontier attitude.

Much more might be said on the pleasanter inheritances from the rural environment—his rather appealing inarticulateness; his dislike of class lines; his warm love of nature, and the feeling for wild life that made him build shelters for rabbits, grow corn for crows, and keep warm water available all winter in the hope of retaining migratory songbirds in the North. One of the most important parts of his countryman's heritage was his stubborn originality of thought—when he did think. He did not take ideas secondhand, but hammered them out for himself, usually on walks in field and wood. Often the ideas were immature. But sometimes he came up with a concept startling for its novel glint of truth.

Like other untutored men, he had a deep suspicion of the uncomprehended, a strong inclination to prejudice, and susceptibility to bad counsel. His antagonism to Wall Street was largely simple distrust of what he did not understand. It is significant that his suspiciousness grew marked when he came under fire. He thought that some newspapers had begun to hound him when he announced the $5 day, and others when he battled for peace and the League of Nations.

"A good part of the American press, not all, is not free," he told reporters. "They misquoted me, distorted what I said, made up lies." The malicious attitude of part of the press toward Ford's Peace Ship, the aspersions on his motives in lifting wages from $2.25 to $5 a day, the attacks on his son Edsel as an alleged draft-dodger, the storm of ridicule accompanying his Senatorial campaign and his libel suit against the Chicago *Tribune* (which he won, with an award of 6¢ in damages) were indeed outrageous. Because Ford was a sensitive man, they converted his early idealism into cynicism. Had he had more education, poise, and perspective, he would not only have avoided some of the occasions for ridicule; he would have met ridicule with a heavier armor.

Out of his sense of needing an agency for

Henry Ford and his son Edsel stand in front of the 10,000,000th car, produced in 1924.

defense and for stating his ideas came the Dearborn *Independent*. Out of his ignorance and suspiciousness came the lamentable anti-Semitic campaign of that weekly, for which he apologized only after vast harm had been done. In this unhappy crusade he had collaborators. E. G. Pipp, who resigned as editor rather than share in it, frankly said to Ford's spokesman, W. J. Cameron, "You are furnishing the brains, Ford the money, and E. G. Liebold the prejudices." Cameron and Liebold furnished some of the methods, too, but as Liebold says, "As long as Mr. Ford wanted it done, it was done." The responsibility was Ford's. That he had no deep-seated race prejudices, but really believed in a fictitious bogy called the International Jew, does not palliate his offense. This, like the shortsighted harshness toward labor organizations, was the abortion of an uninformed mind and uncultivated spirit.

Some aspects of the man remain wholly inexplicable. Highly diffident in some ways, he had an irrepressible desire to be oracular about topics of which he knew nothing. Kindly in most personal relations, he nevertheless countenanced such cruel treatment of subordinates as the smashing of their desks in token of discharge. At times he indulged a good-humored liking for horseplay; at other times he was sternly unapproachable. Sharply practical, he yet cherished some curious superstitions. A churchgoing Episcopalian, he leaned strongly to an unorthodox belief in metempsychosis, or transmigration of souls. There was always something in him of an urchin—a wry, cross-grained, brilliant adolescent.

Yet in this fascinating personality, we come back always to the image of the artist. Much that is otherwise puzzling becomes comprehensible if we think of him in that way—struggling, despite many limitations and handicaps, to remake his world a little nearer to the heart's desire. He wanted to abolish war ("a habit, and a filthy habit," he said), and thus the great gesture of the Peace Ship. He wanted to exclude drink, class divisions, idleness, and disorder. He wanted to get rid of money as

anything but a part of the mechanism of production—"part of the assembly line," or "the connecting rod."

Perhaps his poignant failure lay in his relationship to his son, to whom he gave both intense devotion and total incomprehension. Edsel was a man of the finest qualities of character and mind—upright, idealistic, public-spirited, and hard-working. He was highly philanthropic. In the factory, he got on well with others. In the world at large, he had a broader vision than his father. Some of Henry Ford's acts, such as the anti-Jewish campaign, grieved Edsel greatly, though he was too loyal to speak out publicly. Yet the father, while justly proud of him, committed a fundamental error: He tried to make Edsel in his own image. Of course, he failed in his effort, with anguish to both himself and his son. But the attempt was again, in part, an expression of the artist's desire to make the world over to suit his own vision.

As the years pass and we gain perspective, the blunders and misdeeds in Henry Ford's record will arouse less interest. His social primitivism will seem more a part of the general ignorance and gullibility of our adolescent American civilization. His great achievement will loom up as the significant fact of his career. By his labors in bringing mass production to birth, by his gospel of high production, low prices, and large consumption, he became the key figure in a far-reaching revolution. This fumbling artist actually did remold the world according to his vision. Talking with Edsel one day, he said of his great company: "We'll build this as well as we know how, and if we don't use it, somebody will use it. Anything that is good enough will be used." Of few of the industrial path-hewers of his time can it be said that they produced so much that is permanently and profitably usable.

Allan Nevins, the eminent American historian, won two Pulitzer Prizes, for his studies of Grover Cleveland and Hamilton Fish. He was DeWitt Clinton Professor of History at Columbia University for 27 years and also chairman of the advisory board of American Heritage *magazine.*

Volume 13
ENCYCLOPEDIC SECTION

The two-page reference guide below lists the entries by categories. The entries in this section supplement the subject matter covered in the text of this volume. A **cross-reference** (*see*) means that a separate entry appears elsewhere in this section. However, certain important persons and events mentioned here have individual entries in the Encyclopedic Section of another volume. Consult the Index in Volume 18.

AMERICAN STATESMEN AND POLITICIANS

Newton D. Baker
Bernard M. Baruch
William E. Borah
Champ Clark
Calvin Coolidge
James Cox
Charles Curtis
Harry M. Daugherty
J. J. Davis
John W. Davis
Albert B. Fall
Alvan T. Fuller
Harry A. Garfield
Warren G. Harding
Will H. Hays

Herbert Hoover
Edward M. House
Charles Evans Hughes
Henry Cabot Lodge
William G. McAdoo
Walter Hines Page
A. Mitchell Palmer
James A. Reed
Albert C. Ritchie
Alfred E. Smith
Henry C. Wallace
Frank P. Walsh
Thomas J. Walsh
John W. Weeks
Burton K. Wheeler
Woodrow Wilson

ARTISTS

George W. Bellows
James Montgomery Flagg

Childe Hassam
Jonas Lie

BUSINESS AND INVENTION

Bernard M. Baruch
Luther Burbank
Edward L. Doheny
Henry Ford

Marcus M. Garvey
William Green
Samuel Insull
Eddie Rickenbacker
Harry F. Sinclair

JOURNALISM

Franklin P. Adams
James Cox
George Creel
Marcus M. Garvey

Walter Hines Page
Will Rogers
Mark Sullivan
Henry C. Wallace

LITERATURE

Frederick Lewis Allen
Sherwood Anderson
John Burroughs
John Dos Passos

Theodore Dreiser
F. Scott Fitzgerald
Ernest Hemingway
Sinclair Lewis

POLITICAL DEVELOPMENTS

Communist Party
Marcus M. Garvey
Abbott Lawrence Lowell
Thomas Mooney

Nicola Sacco
Sacco-Vanzetti case
Teapot Dome
Bartolomeo Vanzetti

THE PRESIDENCY

Calvin Coolidge
Warren G. Harding

Herbert Hoover
Woodrow Wilson

THOUGHT AND CULTURE

Bonnie and Clyde
Clara Bow
Charlie Chaplin
George M. Cohan
Jack Dempsey
Greta Garbo
Elinor Glyn
Red Grange

Will H. Hays
Izzie and Moe
Al Jolson
Abbott Lawrence Lowell
Will Rogers
Babe Ruth
Gene Tunney
Rudolph Valentino
Florenz Ziegfeld

WORLD WAR I

American Expeditionary Force
Georges Clemenceau
George Creel
David Lloyd George
Kellogg-Briand Pact
Lusitania
William G. McAdoo
Vittorio Orlando

John J. Pershing
Manfred von Richthofen
Eddie Rickenbacker
Treaty of Versailles
Wilhelm II
Alvin York
Arthur Zimmermann
Zimmermann note

A

ADAMS, Franklin Pierce (1881–1960). A pioneer newspaper columnist and radio personality, "F.P.A." was for many years one of America's best-known humorists. His "Conning Tower," a daily column of wit, verse, and satirical commentary, appeared in New York newspapers for several decades, and he was a panelist on the popular radio program "Information Please" from 1938 to 1948. Adams spent a year at the University of Michigan before turning to journalism in his native Chicago, where his first column appeared in the *Journal* in 1903. Moving to New York City the following year, he wrote for the *Evening Mail* from 1904 to 1913 and then authored "The Conning Tower" while on the staff of the *Tribune* (1913–1921), the *World* (1922–1931), the renamed *Herald-Tribune* (1931–1937), and the *Post* (1938–1941). Adams frequently used his column as a showcase for the work of such rising young writers as **Sinclair Lewis** (*see*), Ring Lardner (1885–1933), and Dorothy Parker (1893–1967). Adams' Saturday column, a review of the week's events, was published in 1935 as *The Diary of Our Own Samuel Pepys: 1911–1934*. He compiled many of his newspaper writings into books, among them *Tobogganing on Parnassus* (1910), *Christopher Columbus* (1931), and *Nods and Becks* (1944). A collector of miscellaneous data and humorous trivia with which he sprinkled his writing and radio patter, Adams also translated Latin poets, collaborated with O. Henry (1862–1910) on the musical comedy *Lo* in 1909, and collected a *Book of Quotations* (1952). Adams wrote little in his last years, contending that "the only people who like

to write [are] the people who write terribly."

ALLEN, Frederick Lewis (1890–1954). An editor and author, Allen specialized in writing informal histories of the United States. Allen, who was born in Boston, was a graduate of Harvard and taught there briefly. He worked on the staffs of the *Atlantic Monthly* (1914–1916), *Century Magazine* (1916–1917), and *Harper's Magazine* (1923–1953). He became editor of *Harper's* in 1941. Inspired by the "tremendous trifles" of the 1920s, Allen wrote a social history of the period entitled *Only Yesterday* (1931). A sequel was written about the 1930s and called *Since Yesterday* (1941). Allen also was the author of *The Lords of Creation* (1935), which covered American financial progress since the 1890s; a biography of John Pierpont Morgan (1837–1913) in 1949; and *The Big Change* (1952), a chronicle of the first half of the 20th century. In addition, he wrote commentaries for two anthologies of photographs.

AMERICAN EXPEDITIONARY FORCE. The nearly 2,000,000 American soldiers who served in Europe during World War I were known as the American Expeditionary Force (A.E.F.). They were commanded by General **John J. Pershing,** who was appointed by President **Woodrow Wilson** (*see both*) after the United States entered the war on April 6, 1917. Pershing at first estimated that 3,000,000 American troops would be necessary to prosecute the war successfully "over there" and believed, like others, that the war would last until 1920. By the time of the Armistice on November 11, 1918, about 2,000,000 doughboys had been transported abroad. Most American troops were engaged against the Germans in eastern France, with a few seeing limited action in Italy. Although the first doughboys began arriving in France in June, 1917, it was almost a year before American forces played a significant role in the fighting. Initially, some Americans were assigned to British and French units, but Pershing, with the backing of Wilson, insisted upon an independent American army. Supply and training problems were gradually overcome, and the Americans—whose very presence was a morale booster to the Allies—soon reached fighting form. In March, 1918, the Germans launched a mighty of-

Flags flying, First Division troops return from the front in France in 1918.

fensive, and by May they were threatening Paris. That June, in the first major American engagement, about 28,000 soldiers of the A.E.F. repulsed the German onslaught at Chateau-Thierry and Belleau Wood. The following month, at the Second Battle of the Marne, the A.E.F. helped halt the German advance and then mounted a massive counterattack involving 270,000 United States soldiers. In August and September, half a million troops of the American First Army smashed the Germans at St.-Mihiel. During the final campaign of the war—the bitterly fought, 47-day Meuse-Argonne offensive that began in late September, 1918—1,200,000 soldiers of the First and Second Armies drove into the almost impenetrable Argonne Forest. With the Allies advancing on all fronts and her own allies collapsing, Germany sued for peace that November. American casualties during the war included 48,909 killed in battle and 63,523 who died from such diseases as influenza and pneumonia. More than 230,000 troops were wounded. The last major American units departed Europe for home the following August.

ANDERSON, Sherwood (1876–1941). A novelist, short-story writer, and poet, Anderson established his reputation as a literary realist with the publication of *Winesburg, Ohio*. This collection of stories, published in 1919, shattered the myth of the sweet, simple life in small-town America. Anderson's boyhood in the town of Clyde, Ohio, furnished him with both the material and locale for much of his adult writing. He left school at 14 to drift from job to job, arriving in Chicago in 1896, where he worked as a laborer. After brief service in the Spanish-American War, he became an

advertising man in Chicago for several years and then managed a paint factory in Elyria, Ohio. One day in 1912, Anderson suddenly walked out of his factory and disappeared. He was found four days later, and after being hospitalized briefly, gave up business to become a writer. Encouraged by Chicago authors **Theodore Dreiser** (*see*) and Carl Sandburg (1878–1967), he brought out *Windy McPherson's Son* (1916), *Marching Men* (1917), and a volume of poems, *Mid-American Chants* (1918). With *Winesburg, Ohio*, his classic treatment of Midwestern drabness and rigidity, Anderson reached the high point of his artistic achievement. Although most of his writings were quite popular, only *Dark Laughter* (1925) became a best seller. Anderson's own life often exhibited the confusion of his fictional characters. He was married four times and moved frequently from one town to the next. In 1926, he finally settled near Troutdale, Virginia, where he published two weekly newspapers, one Democratic and the other Republican. Some of Anderson's best short stories are contained in *The Triumph of the Egg* (1921), *Horses and Men* (1923), and *Death in the Woods* (1933). Among his other important novels are *Poor White* (1920) and *Many Marriages* (1923). Two other books, *A Story Teller's Story* (1924) and *Tar: A Midwest Childhood* (1926), are regarded as largely autobiographical.

B

BAKER, Newton Diehl (1871–1937). A noted American politician and lawyer, Baker was Secretary of War (1916–1921) under President **Woodrow Wilson** (*see*). While he was Secre-

tary during World War I, the army was enlarged from 95,000 men to 4,000,000 and the War Department was reorganized. Born in West Virginia, Baker graduated from Johns Hopkins University in 1892 and became a lawyer two years later. Soon afterward, he joined a law firm in Cleveland, Ohio, where his abilities were quickly recognized by that city's noted reform mayor, Tom Loftin Johnson (1854–1911). Baker subsequently became assistant director of Cleveland's legal department and then served (1902–1912) as city solicitor. He played a significant role in the mayor's battle to lower the fare on the city's transit lines. As mayor of Cleveland himself (1912–1916), Baker continued Johnson's reform policies. Among other achievements, he constructed a municipal electric-power plant. Baker helped secure Wilson's nomination by the Democratic Party in 1912. When Lindsey M. Garrison (1864–1932) resigned as Secretary of War in 1916 in a dispute with Wilson over preparing the nation for possible entry into World War I, Wilson appointed Baker to the post. Although Baker's war achievements were impressive, he was also the object of considerable criticism and was blamed—probably unjustly—for the lack of equipment, clothes, weapons, and facilities at army camps. He was one of Wilson's most trusted confidants. After the war, Baker returned to his law practice in Cleveland. In 1928, he was appointed a member of the Hague Tribunal.

BARUCH, Bernard Mannes (1870–1965). A famous financier, economist, and statesman, Baruch served as an adviser to every President from **Woodrow Wilson** (*see*) to Harry S. Truman (1884–1972) and became known as the nation's elder statesman.

Born in South Carolina, Baruch made a large fortune on the stock market before he was 30. He joined Wilson's administration during World War I as an adviser on national defense and as a member of various war commissions, including the one responsible for making purchases for the Allies. However, his most important service was as chairman of the War Industries Board (1918–1919), a position that gave

Bernard M. Baruch

him control of American industrial production and made him virtual economic dictator of the nation. After the war, Baruch was a member of the economic section of the American commission to negotiate the peace, and during the ensuing negotiations he represented the United States on the reparations and economic commissions. Under **Warren G. Harding** (*see*), Baruch served as a member of the President's Agricultural Conference in 1922. With Harding's successor, **Calvin Coolidge** (*see*), Baruch maintained an informal advisory position, although Coolidge followed little of his advice. Later, Baruch, one of the few people who foresaw the Wall Street crash, helped **Herbert Hoover** (*see*) set up the Reconstruction Finance Corporation in an early attempt to stem the Great Depression. At the request of Franklin D. Roosevelt (1882–1945) during World War

II, Baruch headed a commission to investigate the synthetic-rubber situation in America, and in 1943 he became a special adviser to James F. Byrnes (1879–1972), the director of war mobilization, and also prepared a report on postwar readjustment plans. As the American representative to the United Nations Atomic Energy Commission (1946–1947), he formulated the Baruch Plan for international control of atomic energy, but the proposal was rejected by the Security Council. Baruch was also a philanthropist and the author of several books, including a two-part autobiography, *Baruch: My Story* (1954) and *The Public Years* (1960).

BELLOWS, George Wesley (1882–1925). This artist and lithographer is best known for his scenes of prizefights (*see p. 1150*). Bellows was born in Columbus, Ohio. He graduated from Ohio State University in 1903 and went to New York the next year to study oil painting under Robert Henri (1865–1929). Although Bellows never visited Europe, the prints and paintings of such early realists as Goya (1746–1828) and Daumier (1808–1879) had a profound influence upon his work. In 1907, his *Forty-Two Kids*, depicting boys bathing along New York's riverfront, was Bellows' first canvas to win wide acclaim. The same year, he caused a sensation in art circles with his powerfully animated painting of a prizefight, entitled *Stag at Sharkey's*. In 1909, Bellows became the youngest artist to attain membership in the National Academy of Design. The following year, he taught at the Art Students League in New York City, and he helped organize the famous Armory Show there in 1913. About 1915, Bellows broadened his subject matter to include

landscapes. The next year, he began experimenting with lithography, and during the last nine years of his life he produced prints and book illustrations that became as highly esteemed as his paintings.

BONNIE AND CLYDE. Bonnie Parker (1912?–1934) and Clyde Barrow (1910–1934), two small-time bank robbers, were killed by a posse near Arcadia, Louisiana, and their brief, murderous career was quickly forgotten, until a popular 1968 movie, *Bonnie and Clyde,* revived public interest. The film glamorized the pair and resulted in a gangster-and-gun-moll clothing fad. Texas-born Clyde was 21 and newly paroled from prison when he met the 19-year-old Mrs. Parker on a Dallas street. Shortly thereafter, the couple embarked on a series of bloody robberies in several states. At various times, their accomplices included a teenager named Henry Methvin and Clyde's older brother and sister-in-law, Buck and Blanche Barrow. The Barrow gang received national publicity in April, 1933, when a police raiding party missed the gang but seized snapshots of the criminals posing with their weapons, and a half-finished poem by Bonnie, entitled "The Story of Suicide Sal." Three months later, the police attacked the gang near Platte City, Missouri. Buck Barrow was killed and his wife captured. On May 23, 1934, an ambush was arranged with the help of young Methvin's terrified father, whose farm the gang was using as a hideout. A six-man posse waited as Bonnie and Clyde drove up and stopped to talk with the elder Methvin. Ordered to surrender, Clyde reached for a shotgun, and the police killed them both. Despite the sympathetic film portrayal, the gang was composed of thugs who killed 13 people and whose most successful robbery netted a mere $1,500.

BORAH, William Edgar (1865–1940). A prominent Republican Senator from Idaho, Borah was one of the leaders of the Senate group known as the irreconcilables, who after World War I favored complete rejection of the **Treaty of Versailles** (*see*) because they opposed American membership in the League of Nations. Born in Illinois, Borah became a lawyer in 1887 and soon after made a name for himself as a criminal lawyer in Idaho. In 1907, he won national acclaim as special prosecutor in the trial of William "Big Bill" Haywood (1869–1928) and two other labor leaders, though they were ultimately acquitted of conspiracy in the 1905 murder of former Governor Frank D. Steunenberg of Idaho. Borah was elected to the Senate following the trial and served (1907–1940) in it until his death. A political maverick famous for his independent stands, he was one of the Senate's most eloquent speakers and was sometimes called the Great Opposer. A proponent of states' rights, he opposed both big business and a strong federal government. Besides supporting many labor reforms, Borah led the campaigns in 1913 for the ratification of both the Sixteenth Amendment, which authorized the income tax, and the Seventeenth Amendment, which provided for the direct election of Senators. However, he opposed most of the progressive measures initiated by President **Woodrow Wilson** (*see*), including the Nineteenth Amendment, which gave women the right to vote when it was adopted in 1919. Borah was responsible for calling the Washington Conference of 1921, which brought about the naval disarmament of major world powers. As chairman (1924–1933) of the Senate Foreign Relations Committee, he exerted a tremendous influence on American

policy. He advocated recognition of the Soviet Union but opposed American intervention in Latin America and American membership in the World Court. Borah was also influential in bringing about the **Kellogg-Briand Pact** (*see*) of 1928, which was designed to outlaw war. A leader of Senate isolationists in the 1930s, Borah opposed American intervention in World War II.

BOW, Clara (1905–1965). Best known to millions of moviegoers as the "It" Girl, Miss

ERIC BENSON

Clara Bow

Bow was a silent-screen star of the Jazz Age. The Brooklyn-born actress reached the height of her popularity after **Elinor Glyn** (*see*) used "It" to describe Miss Bow's feminine appeal (*see p. 1158*). Films in which she displayed "It" included *Dangerous Curves, Her Wedding Night, Three Weekends,* and *The Fleet's In.* In 1931, Miss Bow married Rex Bell (1903–1963), an actor. She later participated in his unsuccessful campaign for the governorship of Nevada in 1958.

BURBANK, Luther (1849–1926). This horticulturalist created more than 900 new varieties of flowers,

fruits, vegetables, grains, and grasses. Raised on a farm in Lancaster, Massachusetts, Burbank had little formal education but gained a firsthand knowledge of plants. In 1868, he read *Variation of Animals and Plants Under Domestication* by Charles Darwin (1809–1882), and decided to devote himself to developing new strains of plant life. He opened a market garden near Lunenberg, Massachusetts, and there he developed his first and most famous discovery, the Burbank potato, in 1873. Two years later, Burbank moved to Santa Rosa, California, where he established a nursery garden and greenhouse for his experiments. During the next 50 years, he raised thousands of plants and developed, among others, 40 new varieties of plums and prunes, 10 new berries, the Shasta daisy, and new species of poppies, roses, lilies, tomatoes, apples, peaches, corn, and squash. Once a new plant was under cultivation, Burbank did not preserve his data on it. Thus, many of his methods can only be guessed at by modern scientists. In his lifetime, Burbank published descriptive catalogues and an eight-volume work, *How Plants Are Trained to Work for Man* (1921).

BURROUGHS, John (1837–1921). Burroughs was a writer who specialized in nature essays and poems. Born in upstate New York, he began teaching school in 1854. Nine years later, he moved to Washington, D.C., where he took a position as a clerk in the Treasury Department. That same year, Burroughs' most celebrated poem, "Waiting" (1863), appeared in *Knickerbocker Magazine*. While living in the capital, he became a close friend and devoted admirer of Walt Whitman (1819–1892). His affection for the poet was expressed in his first book, *Notes on Walt Whitman as Poet and Person,* published in 1867. It was followed four years later by *Wake-Robin,* his first work on natural history. In 1873, Burroughs resigned his Treasury job and moved to a small fruit farm near Esopus, New York. During the next 48 years, he devoted himself to nature study and writing. He published about 25 additional books, among them *Winter Sunshine* (1875); his only book of poetry, *Bird and Bough* (1906); and *Field and Study* (1919). His essays on nature, vivid and charming in style, established the nature essay as a literary form. Respected as a naturalist and sage, Burroughs counted many prominent people among his friends. He enjoyed camping trips with President Theodore Roosevelt (1858–1919) and the naturalist John Muir (1838–1914). He was also a friend of Andrew Carnegie (1835–1919) and **Henry Ford** (*see*).

C

CHAPLIN, Charles Spencer ("Charlie") (born 1889). A pantomimist, actor, and film producer, Charlie Chaplin is best known for his silent-movie portrayal of a wistful, cane-swinging tramp who wore a tight frock coat, baggy trousers, bowler hat, and oversized shoes. The London-born entertainer began his career in British vaudeville. In 1910, he accompanied the Karno Comedy Company to New York and for the next three years toured America and Canada with the company. During a performance in New York City, Chaplin was seen by film producer Mack Sennett (1884–1960) and asked to appear in Sennett's famous Keystone Cops comedies. One of the most popular films he made for Sennett was *Tillie's Punc-*

tured Romance. Chaplin developed the character of the tramp in a succession of one- and two-reelers, among them *Easy Street, The Cure,* and *The Tramp.* In 1918, he established the Charlie Chaplin Film Company and began producing films in his own studios. The same year, he released his first independent

Charlie Chaplin

movie, *Shoulder Arms.* It was followed in 1920 by his first full-length film, *The Kid.* That same year, Chaplin joined with Mary Pickford (1893–1979), Douglas Fairbanks, Sr. (1883–1939), and D. W. Griffith (1875–1948) to form United Artists Corporation. Thereafter, Chaplin made *The Pilgrim, The Gold Rush, City Lights,* and *Modern Times.* His first complete talkie, *The Great Dictator,* appeared in 1940. After World War II, he released *Monsieur Verdoux* (1947) and *Limelight* (1952). Chaplin was barred

from reentering the United States in 1952 for refusing to defend his pro-Soviet political views before a Congressional committee. The following year, he established residence in Switzerland with his fourth wife, Oona O'Neill, daughter of the playwright Eugene O'Neill (1888–1953). Later, he produced two films—*A King in New York* (1957), which satirized Congressional investigations and was barred from United States theaters, and the comedy *A Countess From Hong Kong* (1967). Chaplin published *My Autobiography* in 1964.

CLARK, Champ (1850–1921). A power in the Democratic Party during the early part of the 20th century, Clark was a Representative from Missouri for 26 years (1893–1895 and 1897–1921) and was Speaker of the House from 1911 to 1919. He nearly captured the Democratic nomination for the Presidency in 1912 but was passed over when party leader William Jennings Bryan (1860–1925) shifted his support to **Woodrow Wilson** (*see*). A native of Kentucky, Clark as a youth changed his given name from James Beauchamp to Champ. He was educated at Kentucky University, Bethany College in West Virginia, and the Cincinnati Law School. After receiving his law degree in 1875, he resided for a year in Kansas and then moved to Missouri, where he practiced law and edited newspapers in small towns. A noted orator—his speech was usually more forceful than polite—Clark served in the Missouri legislature (1889–1891) before entering Congress. He rose steadily in influence, becoming the Democratic leader in the House by 1907. In 1910, Clark helped to break the power of the reactionary Republican Speaker, Joseph G. "Uncle Joe" Cannon (1836–1926), and he himself became Speaker the next year. Clark supported the Spanish-American War in 1898. However, he strongly opposed the Selective Draft Act of 1917 during World War I. Clark was defeated for reelection in 1920, the same year he published his autobiography, *My Quarter Century of American Politics.*

CLEMENCEAU, Georges (1841–1929). As premier of France, Clemenceau headed the French delegation to the Paris Peace Conference in 1919 (*see p. 1103*). His primary interest was his nation's security, and he arrived in Versailles demanding measures that would keep Germany weak. As a young man, Clemenceau had fled to America in 1865 during the reign of Napoleon III (1808–1873). He worked as a journalist and teacher until it was safe to return to France in 1869. There, he embarked upon a stormy political career that eventually led to his serving as premier from 1906 to 1909. In the midst of World War I in 1917, Clemenceau, who was known as the Tiger, was called upon to form a coalition cabinet. He did, with the motto, "The war and nothing but the war." After Germany's defeat, Clemenceau was chairman of the Peace Conference, whose main participants included President **Woodrow Wilson,** British Prime Minister **David Lloyd George,** and Italian Premier **Vittorio Orlando** (*see all*). At first, he demanded heavy reparations and the cession to France of the left bank of the Rhine and the industrial Saar Basin, both German-inhabited areas. These issues and Clemenceau's forceful personality made him Wilson's chief antagonist at the conference. Clemenceau believed that Wilson was an idealist who was unaware of the realities of Europe. Clemenceau was forced to give ground on his demands. The Saar was put under

Georges Clemenceau

French economic control for only 15 years, and the Rhineland was left to Germany as a demilitarized zone. Clemenceau always regarded the **Treaty of Versailles** (*see*) as inadequate for the future security of France. Because of the treaty, he was defeated in his bid for the presidency in 1920. Afterward, he devoted himself to writing and lecturing, touring America for four months in 1920 and 1921.

COHAN, George Michael (1878–1942). A prolific songwriter and playwright, Cohan was the composer of the popular World War I song *Over There* as well as one of the most popular performers of his day. The entertainer first appeared on stage at the age of nine in *Daniel Boone.* At 13, he starred in *Peck's Bad Boy.* From 1890 to 1900, he toured the vaudeville circuit with his parents and sister in an act billed as "The Four Cohans." By the time he was 15, Cohan was writing songs and skits for the act. In 1901, he made his Broadway debut in his own play, *The Governor's Son.* Three years later, he went into partnership with the

producer Sam H. Harris (1872–1941). They produced more than 50 plays, revues, and musicals during almost 15 years together. Among them were *Little Johnny Jones* (1904), *Forty-five Minutes from Broadway* (1905), *George Washington, Jr.* (1906), *The Man Who Owns Broadway* (1908), *Get-Rich-Quick Wallingford* (1910), and *Seven Keys to Baldpate* (1913). Cohan also acted in plays other than his own, including *Ah, Wilderness* (1932), by Eugene O'Neill (1888–1953), and *I'd Rather Be Right* (1937), by George S. Kaufman (1889–1961) and Moss Hart (1904–1961). He wrote lyrics and music for countless songs. Besides *Over There,* he is perhaps best remembered for the patriotic tune *It's a Grand Old Flag.* A film, *Yankee Doodle Dandy* (1942), and a Broadway musical, *George M* (1968), were based on his life. A statue of Cohan was erected in Duffy Square, in the heart of the Broadway theater district, in 1959.

COMMUNIST PARTY. Although there had been Communists in the United States who had followed the teachings of the German political theorists Karl Marx (1818–1883) and Friedrich Engels (1820–1895) since their *Communist Manifesto* was published in 1847, no organized movement was formed until 1919, two years after the Bolshevik Revolution in Russia. At that time, dissatisfied members of the Socialist Party, demanding more active efforts to overthrow the capitalist economic system and institute state socialism, organized both the Communist Party of America and the Communist Labor Party. From the beginning, the movement was divided, with rival factions contending for power, and the party has been frequently reorganized and renamed. In general, American communism has followed the leadership of the Soviet Union. The "party line" has changed frequently to conform to changes in Soviet policy. The Communists had no sooner begun to organize than they were driven underground by the "Red scare" of 1919–1920, when Attorney General **A. Mitchell Palmer** (*see*) ordered the mass arrest of political agitators. They surfaced in 1921 as members of the renamed Workers Party of America and in 1924 supported William Z. Foster (1881–1961) in the Presidential election. He received 33,000 votes. That same year, the party began publishing its own newspaper, *The Daily Worker*. Renamed the Communist League of America, the party drew 48,000 votes for

Foster received about 102,000 votes. By the late 1920s, Communists were engaged in an overt campaign to take over the nation's labor movement. The party has always made extensive use of "front" groups to further its aims, and during the Depression it was able to solicit the support of non-Communist "sympathizers" and "fellow travelers." Earl Browder (born 1891) polled 80,000 votes as the party's Presidential candidate in 1936 but could draw only 48,000 in 1940. After supporting the American war effort during World War II, the party reverted to its militant opposition to the nation's social and economic system. Although it ran no candidates for the Presidency in 1948, it backed the

to a series of stringent governmental regulations that gradually undermined its strength. The Smith Act of 1940 made it unlawful to advocate the violent overthrow of the government, and 11 Communist leaders were convicted and imprisoned under this act in 1949. Communist power in labor unions was restricted by the Taft-Hartley Act of 1947, which prohibited Communists from serving as union officials. Party activities were further curtailed by the McCarran Internal Security Act of 1950, the Communist Control Act of 1954, and the "Red hunt" of the early 1950s led by Senator Joseph R. McCarthy (1909–1957) of Wisconsin. Following criticism by Russian leaders of the deceased Soviet dictator Joseph Stalin (1879–1953) and the Hungarian revolution of 1956, a rift developed within the already weakened American Communist ranks from which the party has never recovered. Today, in spite of recent Supreme Court rulings that have eased restrictions on the party, it has a membership in the United States of only about 10,000 persons.

COOLIDGE, (John) Calvin (1872–1933). Although the 30th President of the United States was more an administrator than a leader—advocating a laissez-faire (noninterference) policy in domestic matters and virtual isolationism in foreign policy—his conservative Republicanism was endorsed by the majority of Americans in the decade following World War I. Born in Plymouth Notch, Vermont, "Silent Cal" inherited from his storekeeper father such traditional New England virtues as frugality, taciturnity, industry, honesty, and a lasting respect for business. Graduating from Amherst College in 1895, Coolidge entered a law office in Northamp-

"Reds" arrested in a 1920 roundup are shipped to Ellis Island for deportation.

Foster in 1928. The following year, it was renamed the Communist Party of the United States of America, the title it has retained—except for a short period from 1944 to 1945, when it was called the Communist Political Association. In 1932, in his strongest showing at the polls,

slate of the Progressive Party, which nominated Henry A. Wallace (1888–1965) as its Presidential candidate. With Wallace's defeat in the election that year, communism ceased to be a significant political force in the nation. Beginning in 1940, the Communist Party was subjected ton, Massachusetts. He passed the state bar examinations in 1897 and soon became involved in politics. A staunch Republican from the start, Coolidge progressed steadily up the political ladder. As a state senator (1912–1915), he warned against the dangers of passing too many laws, saying, "It is much more important to kill bad bills than to pass good ones." Coolidge twice served as the governor of Massachusetts (1919–1920), and he became a national figure as a result of his suppressing a Boston police strike in 1919. Widespread rioting and looting had broken out on that city's streets, and a general workers' strike was being threatened after 1,117 out of its 1,544 underpaid policemen had gone on strike. Coolidge called out the state guard and finally restored order, declaring, "There is no right to strike against the public safety by anybody, anywhere, any time." In 1920, the Republican Party chose him to run for Vice-President on the ticket with **Warren G. Harding** (*see*), who won the election. As Vice-President, Coolidge was untouched by the scandals that rocked the Harding administration. After he was elevated to the Presidency on August 3, 1923 upon Harding's death, he got rid of those persons in the cabinet involved in the corrupt oil leases, and he was elected President in his own right in 1924 with nearly 16,000,000 votes, or nearly 7,000,000 more than his Democratic opponent, **John W. Davis** (*see*). Asserting that "the business of America is business," the President adopted domestic policies favorable to big business. These included tax cuts, high tariffs, and immigration restrictions. He refused to allow government interference in private industry and twice vetoed farm-relief bills, saying, "Farmers have never made money, I don't believe we can do much about

it." He lowered the national debt by $2,000,000,000 in three years, but he also hindered the development of natural resources. In foreign affairs, he refused to have anything to do with the League of Nations or the World Court. However, he did back the **Kellogg-Briand Pact** (*see*) of 1928, which was intended to outlaw war. Coolidge did not seek reelection in 1928, giving his support instead to **Herbert Hoover** (*see*), his Secretary of Commerce. Retiring to Northampton, he spent his remaining years writing newspaper and magazine articles. He died of a heart attack on January 5, 1933.

COX, James Middleton (1870–1957). A staunch supporter of the **Treaty of Versailles** (*see*) and the League of Nations, Cox lost the first Presidential election held after World War I to **Warren G. Harding** (*see*). Born in Ohio, Cox worked as an editor and reporter for the Cincinnati *Enquirer*. In 1898, he bought the Dayton *Daily News,* which he merged with the Springfield *Press-Republican* seven years later. This formed the basis of what ultimately became a newspaper empire that included the Atlanta *Journal* and other important dailies. Cox served two terms in the House of Representatives (1909–1913) and three terms as governor of Ohio (1913–1915 and 1917–1921). While governor in 1920, Cox was chosen by the Democratic Party as its Presidential candidate—with Assistant Secretary of the Navy Franklin D. Roosevelt (1882–1945) as his running mate. A supporter of **Woodrow Wilson** (*see*), he ran on a platform that endorsed American ratification of the Treaty of Versailles and promised that, if elected, he would see that America joined the League of Nations as quickly as possible. However, the Re-

publican candidate, Warren G. Harding, triumphed by a landslide and soon made it clear that the United States would never enter the League of Nations. Cox's understanding of business and economics led to his appointment as vice-chairman of the American delegation to the World Economic Conference that met in London in 1933. The conference attempted to increase world trade and considered such measures as tariff reductions and international currency stabilization, but it was not a success. In 1946, Cox published *Journey Through My Years.*

CREEL, George (1876–1953). As civilian chairman of the Committee on Public Information, Creel directed the anti-German propaganda campaign during World War I. The Missouri-born journalist worked briefly for several Midwestern papers before joining the staff of the New York *Journal* in 1898. Two years later, he returned to Missouri, where he helped establish the Kansas City *Independent.* Creel subsequently worked for two Denver papers, the *Post* (1909–1910) and the *Rocky Mountain News* (1911–1913). Immediately after America's entry into World War I in 1917, President **Woodrow Wilson** (*see*) created the Committee on Public Information to arouse public support for the war effort. Creel was appointed chairman of the four-man board. Under his direction, the committee organized a campaign of pamphlets, movies, posters, and news clips designed to arouse anti-German sentiment (*see pp. 1098–1099*). The efforts of journalists, ministers, and scholars were enlisted to help unite public opinion against "the Hun." A patriotic fervor soon swept the nation. Sauerkraut was renamed liberty cabbage, and the eating of pretzels, a tidbit of German origin, was denounced. The excessive patriotism reached the point where men with foreign names were forced to kiss the American flag, and owners of dachshunds and German shepherd dogs were suspected of being enemy sympathizers. Creel was later criticized by some historians for fomenting an excess of patriotism. Later, during the Depression, Creel served as chairman of the San Francisco Regional Labor Board (1933) and chairman of the national advisory committee to the Works Progress Administration (1935).

CURTIS, Charles (1860–1936). A well-known Republican politician, Curtis was Vice-President (1929–1933) during the administration of **Herbert Hoover** (*see*). Born in Kansas, Curtis became a lawyer in 1881 and subsequently specialized in criminal law. He entered politics as county attorney (1885–1889) for Shawnee County, Kansas, and then served in the House of Representatives (1892–1907) and in the Senate (1907–1913 and 1915–1929). In Congress, Curtis was noted for the excellent relations he maintained with his constituents and was considered virtually unbeatable in elections. Although he rarely wrote bills or made speeches, he exerted a considerable influence on legislation as Senate majority leader from 1924 to 1929. Curtis was Hoover's running mate again in 1932, but the ticket was defeated by the Democrats Franklin D. Roosevelt (1882–1945) and John Nance Garner (1868–1967). Curtis subsequently returned to private law practice.

D

DAUGHERTY, Harry Micajah (1860–1941). An Ohio-born lawyer and politician, Daugherty was appointed Attorney General in 1921 by President **Warren G. Harding** (*see*) and was subsequently implicated in several of the scandals of the Harding administration, notably the **Teapot Dome** (*see*). He was forced to resign in March, 1924, by Harding's successor, **Calvin Coolidge** (*see*). Three years later, he was prosecuted for conspiracy to defraud the government but was acquitted after two juries failed to agree. Daugherty, who graduated from the University of Michigan in 1881, practiced law in his native city of Washington Court House, Ohio, until 1893, when he moved to Columbus. There he became a successful corporation lawyer. He served in the Ohio legislature (1890–1894) and was a powerful member of the state Republican Party. Daugherty helped his close friend Harding win the Presidential nomination in 1920. He directed his campaign and was rewarded after Harding's election by an appointment to his cabinet. Daugherty's service as Attorney General (1921–1924) was clouded by hints of corruption. Nevertheless, he was able to collect millions of dollars for the government in prohibition and war-fraud cases, and he established at Chillicothe, Ohio, the first federal prison for first offenders. He also appointed J. Edgar Hoover (born 1895) as head of the Federal Bureau of Investigation. In 1932, Daugherty published *The Inside Story of the Harding Tragedy*, which he wrote with Thomas Dixon (1864–1946).

DAVIS, James John (1873–1947). Davis was a steelworker and a politician who was appointed Secretary of Labor by **Warren G. Harding** (*see*) in 1921 and remained in that post under two other Republican Presidents —**Calvin Coolidge** and **Herbert Hoover** (*see both*). Born in Wales, Davis came to America in 1881 and at the age of 11 went to work as a puddler—a purifier of impure metal—in a Pittsburgh steel and iron plant. He later moved to Elwood, Indiana, where he became interested in local politics and labor activities. In 1906, Davis was appointed director general of the Loyal Order of the Moose, a fraternal organization. Its membership rose to more than 600,000 under his direction, and he became a well-known figure. After serving as Secretary of Labor (1921–1930), he was a Senator from Pennsylvania (1930–1945). Davis described his youth in *The Iron Puddler* (1922).

DAVIS, John William (1873–1955). A compromise Presidential candidate of the Democratic Party in 1924, Davis was thoroughly trounced in the election by Republican **Calvin Coolidge** (*see*). Born in West Virginia, Davis graduated from Washington and Lee University in 1892 and received a law degree three years later. Entering politics, he served in West Virginia's House of Delegates in 1899 and was elected to the United States House of Representatives in 1911. He resigned from Congress two years later upon his appointment as Solicitor General (1913–1918). During World War I, Davis worked as an attorney for the American Red Cross. He also attended a 1918 conference with the German representatives in Berne, Switzerland, to discuss the treatment and exchange of prisoners. After serving as ambassador to Great Britain from 1918 to 1921, Davis became president of the American Bar Association. At the Democratic National Convention in 1924, the Southern wing of the party supported the candidacy of **William G. McAdoo,** while the Northern faction favored New York's governor, **Alfred E. Smith** (*see both*). Davis, a conservative who was allied with important business interests, was chosen as a compromise between the opposing groups. In the election, Davis lost to Coolidge, polling only 8,400,000 votes to the victor's 15,700,000. Although he was a Democrat, in 1936 Davis supported the anti-New Deal Liberty League and the Republican Presidential candidate, Alfred M. Landon (1887–1987). During his career as an attorney, Davis pleaded before the Supreme Court in 140 cases, more than any other lawyer in the nation's history.

DEMPSEY, William Harrison ("Jack") (born 1895). Heavyweight boxing champion of the world from 1919 to 1926, Demp-

Jack Dempsey

sey was the biggest drawing card in the history of prizefighting, attracting more spectators to his matches and earning more money than any other boxer. Jack Dempsey was born in Manassa, Colorado. He became a professional fighter at the age of 18 and had a record of 50 victories against only two defeats by the time of his first title fight six years later. Dempsey won the heavyweight crown after three rounds by a technical knockout over Jess Willard (1883–1968) at Toledo, Ohio, on July 4, 1919. He successfully defended his championship against Georges Carpentier in 1921, and in 1923 against both Tom Gibbons and Luis ("Wild Bull of the Pampas") Firpo (*see p. 1150*). The "Manassa Mauler" lost a 10-round decision to **Gene Tunney** (*see*) in September, 1926, in a fight witnessed by more than 120,000 people in Philadelphia. Attempting to regain the title the following year at Soldiers Field in Chicago, Dempsey was again outboxed by the swift-footed Tunney in the controversial "long count" fight. About 100,000 fans, paying a record $2,600,000, saw Dempsey floor Tunney in the seventh round for an estimated 16 seconds, only to find the apparent knockout disallowed when Dempsey failed to retreat to the neutral corner while Tunney was down. Dempsey retired from the ring in 1928 but returned to box 56 exhibition bouts in 1931 and 1932. A physical training officer in the United States Coast Guard during World War II, Dempsey later opened a popular restaurant in New York City.

DOHENY, Edward. *See* **Teapot Dome.**

DOS PASSOS, John (1896–1970). A prominent novelist and social commentator, Dos Passos is among the originators of documentary fiction—tales based on actual issues and events in 20th-century American life. Dos Pas-

sos was born in Chicago and attended schools in Europe before graduating from Harvard in 1916. He subsequently went to Spain to study architecture, but World War I changed his plans. He joined the French ambulance service and later the United States Medical Corps. After the war, Dos Passos worked as a correspondent and free-lance magazine writer. His war experiences furnished material for *Three Soldiers* (1921), the first of his novels to win critical acclaim. Dos Passos reached his maturity as a writer with *Manhattan Transfer* (1925). This book contains hundreds of diverse episodes that paint a picture of life in the sprawling New York metropolis. During the 1930s, Dos Passos began writing about current social problems— the victims of the Depression, the oppression of workers, and labor disputes. His concern for the little man was worked into *In All Countries* (1934) and *The Big Money* (1936), both of which dealt in part with the **Sacco-Vanzetti case** (*see*). Dos Passos' most famous work, *U.S.A.*, was published in 1938. It is made up of three earlier novels—*The 42nd Parallel* (1930), *1919* (1932), and *The Big Money* —that together present the author's comprehensive view of America between 1900 and 1930. In it, Dos Passos wrote pessimistically about the degradation and exploitation of the individual in a corrupt capitalistic society. The narrative was punctuated by snatches from contemporary headlines, newspaper articles, advertisements, and popular songs, to suggest the general atmosphere of the period. Biographies of prominent Americans were also interspersed in the narrative. Dos Passos published a second trilogy, *District of Columbia*, in 1952. This time, he departed from the radical

John Dos Passos

left-wing philosophy of his earlier years and instead defended the American status quo and condemned communism, fascism, and the New Deal. His later conservatism is also evident in such works as *Midcentury* (1961), which discussed the conflicts of contemporary society, and *Mr. Wilson's War* (1963), which examined the history of the United States from 1901 to 1921.

DREISER, Theodore (1871–1945). A pioneer in the literary movement toward naturalism, Dreiser gave his novels force and significance by writing honest, detailed pictures of American society, uncolored by the romantic attitudes that characterized earlier fiction. Dreiser, the son of poor, devoutly religious parents, grew up in Indiana yearning for material comforts. After spending a year at the University of Indiana, he worked as a newspaper reporter in Chicago, St. Louis, and Pittsburgh from 1892 to 1894. He then moved to New York City, where he was a freelance writer and journalist until 1910. *Sister Carrie* (1900)—his first novel and sometimes considered his greatest—is the story of a working girl who becomes a

theater star, while her socially respectable lover ends up living in squalor. The novel met with such a storm of protest from critics because of its frankness about "immorality" that the publisher, Doubleday, Page & Company, withdrew it from publication after 1,000 copies had been printed but not distributed. (*Sister Carrie* was finally republished in 1912.) As a result, Dreiser became a lifelong opponent of censorship. He continued to be criticized for not condemning the immorality of the characters in his works until 1925, when his most famous novel, *An American Tragedy*, was published. A best seller, it was based on a 1906 case of murder by drowning, with only the names of its main characters changed. The novel expressed Dreiser's philosophy that men are the victims of social and economic forces. It also condemned American society for its rigid moral standards and emphasis on material success. Following a visit to Russia in 1927, Dreiser embraced socialism, and his writings after that time reflect this. A trilogy about the rise to power of an unscrupulous business magnate—*The Financier* (1912), *The Titan* (1914), and *The Stoic* (1947)—was written over a period of 35 years. In addition to novels, Dreiser also wrote several autobiographies, essays, poems, short stories, and studies of real persons, including one of his older brother, the popular song-writer Paul Dresser (1857–1906).

F

FALL, Albert B. *See* **Teapot Dome.**

FITZGERALD, Francis Scott Key (1896–1940). F. Scott Fitzgerald chronicled the manners, morals, and mood of the Jazz Age of the 1920s, often basing his novels and short stories on his own tragic life. A native of St. Paul, Minnesota, Fitzgerald entered Princeton University in 1913, where he socialized with the rich and prominent youths who later figured in his novels. After dropping out of Princeton for a year because of bad grades, Fitzgerald returned briefly but then enlisted in the army in 1917. While training in Alabama, he began his first novel, *This Side of Paradise,* which was set in Princeton and which captured the mood of prewar America. Upon its publication in 1920, Fitzgerald became rich and famous. That same year, he married Zelda Sayre (1900–1947). Much like the swingers he wrote about, the couple lived extravagantly (*see p. 1160*). The early years of their marriage were echoed in his second novel, *The Beautiful and Damned* (1921). In what is considered his masterpiece, *The Great Gatsby* (1925), Fitzgerald dealt with the themes of romantic love, infidelity, and violence and depicted the elusiveness of the "American dream" in his contemporaries' lives. The Fitzgeralds, who had lived in Europe since 1924, began drinking heavily, and their marriage deteriorated because of frequent quarrels. When Zelda suffered a mental breakdown in 1930, they returned to America. Fitzgerald recorded the tragedy of their marriage in the semiautobiographical novel *Tender Is the Night* (1934). The accumulated burdens of his wife's mental disintegration, their growing debts, and the loss of his own popularity caused Fitzgerald to fear that his talent was dead. He revealed this fear in several deeply moving essays written about this time. They were published posthumously in a collection entitled *The Crack Up*

(1945). In need of money, Fitzgerald went to Hollywood in 1937, where he wrote movie scripts and worked on another novel. But he was unable to complete *The Last Tycoon*—the story of a Hollywood mogul—before his death in 1940, though the book was published in unfinished form a year later.

FLAGG, James Montgomery (1877–1960). Flagg was an illustrator best remembered for his World War I recruiting poster of a stern Uncle Sam pointing toward the viewer and saying, "I Want You" (*see front endsheet*). Born in upstate New York, Flagg was only 12 years old when he sold his first drawings to *St. Nicholas Magazine*. He later studied at the Art Students League in New York City, and in England and Paris. Flagg's illustrations were published in such leading magazines as *Life* and *Cosmopolitan*. During World War I, he designed many patriotic posters. The celebrated one of Uncle Sam, which Flagg himself posed for, was originally designed as a cover for *Leslie's Illustrated*. More than 4,000,000 copies of it were distributed during World War I and World War II. Flagg also painted portraits, drew a syndicated comic strip, and published a number of books, including his autobiography, *Buckshot and Roses* (1946). In 1920, Flagg joined the Society of Illustrators and was a founder of the Dutch Treat Club, a New York club for illustrators and actors.

FORD, Henry (1863–1947). Ford was an industrialist who pioneered in automotive production (*see pp. 1162–1168*). The Michigan-born manufacturer left his father's farm at the age of 16 to become an apprentice in a Detroit machine shop. He later worked as an engineer for the

Edison Illuminating Company. In 1896, Ford built his first gasoline-driven "horseless carriage." His dream, however, was to produce an efficient, inexpensive automobile in mass quantity. After organizing the Ford Motor Company in 1907, he concentrated on the development of assembly-line production. By cutting production costs, he was able to manufacture the first low-priced, standardized car, the popular Model T, in 1908. Three years later, after a long litigation, Ford won a patent suit that liberated the entire automobile industry from the licensing claims of George B. Selden (1846–1922), an early automobile designer. As profits rose, Ford established a profit-sharing plan, an eight-hour day, and a minimum daily wage of $5 for his employees—measures that caused a sensation in 1914. A pacifist, Ford led a privately sponsored peace expedition to Norway in 1915 in an attempt to end World War I. However, after America entered the war, the industrialist converted his plants to military production. Urged by President **Woodrow Wilson** (*see*), Ford ran for the Senate as a Democrat in 1918. He was narrowly defeated by Truman H. Newberry (1864–1945), who was forced to resign in 1922 because of his corrupt practices in that election. Ford's election would have given the Democratic Party a majority in the Senate during the crucial debates on the League of Nations. In 1922, Ford purchased the Lincoln Motor Company. Thereafter, he manufactured higher-priced cars in addition to the Model T. In 1926, Ford introduced the five-day week, and under pressure from his son Edsel Ford (1893–1943), replaced the outmoded Model T with the Model A the following year. Paternalistic toward his employees, Ford was opposed to

labor unions. As a result, the company did not recognize a union until 1941, after a series of bloody strikes led by Walter Reuther (1907–1970). These strikes and Ford's refusal to introduce basic technological improvements pressed by his son Edsel brought a decline of the company, which even large defense contracts during World War II could not check. The elder Ford resigned in 1945 and was replaced by his grandson Henry Ford II (1917–1987), who brought about the revival of the company. The Ford Foundation, established in 1936 by Edsel Ford, has given approximately $7,000,000,000 to educational and social programs.

FULLER, Alvan Tufts (1878–1958). This governor of Massachusetts is best remembered for his role in setting up a commission to judge the fairness of the verdict in the controversial **Sacco-Vanzetti case** (*see*). Born in Boston, Fuller was educated in public schools and began working in the bicycle business in 1896. He subsequently pioneered in the infant automobile industry, becoming a founder and owner of the Packard Motor Company in Boston. As a Republican, he was elected to the Massachusetts legislature in 1915 and then served two terms in the House of Representatives (1917–1921). He became lieutenant governor of Massachusetts in 1921 and ran successfully for governor in 1924 and 1926. It was during his second term in office that Fuller bowed to popular demand for a review of the trial of Nicola Sacco (1891–1927) and Bartolomeo Vanzetti (1888–1927), two Italian immigrants who were accused of murder. On June 1, 1927, Fuller appointed a three-man advisory committee headed by **Abbott Lawrence Lowell** (*see*), president of Harvard, to inquire into the fairness of the defendants' trial. Fuller, meanwhile, conducted a separate study on his own. On August 3, 1927, he and the committee announced their unanimous decision that the trial had been fair. They upheld both the verdict of guilty and the death penalty. Fuller, who was later chairman of the board of the Cadillac-Oldsmobile Company, declined payment for his services while in public office.

G

GARBO, Greta (born 1905). A native of Stockholm, Sweden, "the Divine Garbo" starred in 24 American movies before her retirement in 1941. Her beauty was universally admired, along with her acting ability. Her de-

For her first "talkie," Anna Christie, *Garbo starred with George Marion.*

sire to avoid publicity added an aura of mystery to her image. Born Greta Gustafsson, she planned early to become an actress but first worked as a latherer in a barbershop, as a model, and as a department-store clerk. A chance meeting in a store with a film director led to her first film

role in 1922. Four years later, Miss Garbo starred in her first American movies, *The Torrent* and *The Temptress*. Her first sound movie, widely advertised with the slogan "Garbo Talks," was *Anna Christie* (1930), which established her image as a tragic heroine. Others of her best-known films were *Mata Hari* (1931), *Grand Hotel* (1932), *Anna Karenina* (1935), and her first comedy, *Ninotchka* (1939). Some attribute her retirement to the bad reviews she received in her last film, *Two-Faced Woman* (1941). Miss Garbo's unwillingness to talk in public—"I vant to be alone" became her trademark—was the subject of much publicity during her career. There have been frequent revivals of her films since her retirement.

GARFIELD, Harry Augustus (1863–1942). A son of the 20th President of the United States, James A. Garfield (1831–1881), Harry Garfield was a noted lawyer and educator. Born in Hiram, Ohio, Garfield graduated from his father's alma mater, Williams College, in 1885, and taught for a time at the Saint Paul's School in Concord, New Hampshire. In 1888, he moved to Cleveland, where he practiced law, and from 1891 to 1897 taught at Western Reserve University. Garfield became a professor of politics at Princeton in 1903 and five years later was appointed president of Williams College, a post he held for 26 years (1908–1934). Shortly after the United States entered World War I, President **Woodrow Wilson** (*see*) named Garfield national fuel administrator (1917–1919). Initially, the press blamed Garfield for coal shortages in Ohio and the Northeastern states. However, Congressional investigations disclosed that it was the failure of the railroads to

meet the heavy wartime demand on them that caused the fuel shortage. The railroads were subsequently placed under federal control.

GARVEY, Marcus Moziah (1887–1940). Garvey was one of the earliest and most important black-nationalist leaders in 20th-century America. His famous "Back to Africa" movement of the 1920s was largely unsuccessful, chiefly because few of America's more than 10,000,000 black citizens wanted to resettle in Liberia. Garvey's Universal Negro Improvement Association, founded in 1914, gained an impressive following in its early years but declined steadily after Garvey was charged with fraudulent use of association investment funds and sent to prison in 1925. Garvey was born at St. Ann's Bay, Jamaica, in the British West Indies. He was a Maroon, one of the descendants of escaped slaves whose independence in the hill country of Jamaica was recognized by Britain in 1739. Garvey's education was obtained largely by independent reading, because he was forced to drop out of school at the age of 14 and begin work as a printer's apprentice. After moving to Kingston about 1904, he became a leader of an abortive printers' strike in 1907. Garvey's growing interest in the special problems of blacks found voice in several unsuccessful newspapers he edited in Costa Rica and Panama over the next few years. A two-year stay in London (1912–1914), where he came in contact with African nationalists, furthered his determination to aid his people. Back in Jamaica in 1914, Garvey organized the Universal Negro Improvement Association, an attempt to unify black people and foster pride among them. As head of the association, he liked

Marcus M. Garvey

to appear in public dressed in a resplendent uniform. Transferring his headquarters to New York City after 1916, Garvey published (1918–1923) a weekly newspaper, the *Negro World*. He also started the Negro Factories Corporation to generate new black businesses and in 1919 founded a steamship company, the Black Star Line, to promote trade between New York, Africa, and the West Indies. Garvey's written and oratorical persuasiveness soon drew many thousands of American blacks to join his association and invest in his enterprises. However, when the steamship line suddenly collapsed in 1921, chiefly because of his ineptness in financial matters, its investors lost more than $750,000 and Garvey was indicted for fraud. He was tried and convicted in May, 1923, and was sentenced to five years in the Atlanta, Georgia, penitentiary. His sentence was commuted by President **Calvin Coolidge** (*see*) after he had served two years (1925–1927), but he was deported to Jamaica. Garvey continued his black-nationalist activities the rest of his life, but with diminishing success. He published the periodical

Black Man in London from 1934 until his death in 1940.

GLYN, Elinor Sutherland (1865–1943). Mrs. Glyn was a British novelist who first used "It" to signify sex appeal. She was raised in England, where she married Clayton Glyn, a wealthy landowner, in 1892. Her first novel, *The Visits of Elizabeth,* was published in 1900. It was followed seven years later by *Three Weeks,* a story of passionate love. The latter book, translated into several languages, established her reputation. Thereafter, Mrs. Glyn wrote a succession of romantic novels with such titles as *Man and Maid* (1922), *This Passion Called Love* (1926), *The Flirt and the Flapper* (1930), and *Did She?* (1934). Her books were popular but had little literary merit. However, they did reflect the manners of the period in which they were written. They also mirrored the red-haired author's own quest for romance. As she said of herself, "On looking back at my life I see that the dominant interest, in fact the fundamental impulse behind every action, has been

Elinor Glyn

the desire for *romance*." From 1922 to 1927, Mrs. Glyn resided in Hollywood, where she wrote short stories, novels, and movie scenarios. During this period, she prepared the script for *It,* the film that introduced **Clara Bow** (*see*) as the "It" Girl.

GRANGE, Harold Edward ("Red") (born 1903). The gridiron exploits of Red Grange in the 1920s and 1930s started football on its rise to national popularity. Unprecedented crowds flocked to college and professional games to watch the sensational running ability of "The Galloping Ghost." Grange, a native of Forksville, Pennsylvania, began playing the sport in Wheaton, Illinois, where he averaged five touchdowns a game in his junior year at high school. At the University of Illinois, the red-haired, 5-foot-10, 170-pound speedster was an All-American halfback in 1923, 1924, and 1925, scoring 31 touchdowns in 20 games during his college career and gaining more than 4,000 yards by running and passing. In one contest against Michigan in 1924, Red scored on runs of 92, 70, 57, and 43 yards the first four times he handled the ball—all in the first quarter. He tallied again on a 64-yard gallop later in the game and passed for another touchdown. Grange started a great furor when he signed a professional contract after graduation, because play-for-pay football was then considered somewhat disreputable. However, he revolutionized the sport, and for one game alone—at the Polo Grounds in New York in 1925—he drew 73,000 fans, or four times the average game attendance. Grange played with the Chicago Bears for a year before joining in 1926 the New York Yankees, a team formed especially around him. When injuries forced him to quit in 1927, he went to Hollywood and appeared in several movies. Grange returned to the Bears in 1929 and played six more seasons with them before his retirement in 1935. During his professional career, Grange averaged 8.1 yards per carry and scored 531 touchdowns.

GREEN, William (1873–1952). As president of the American Federation of Labor (1924–1952), Green was a conservative who was praised by some as being conciliatory and condemned by others for being timid. He toned down the militancy of organized labor and sought closer cooperation with management and the federal government. Beginning as a worker in the coal mines of his native Ohio, Green rose through a series of regional posts in the United Mine Workers of America to become national secretary-treasurer of that union (1912–1924). While serving as a Democratic senator in the state legislature (1910–1913), he was instrumental in securing passage of the Ohio Workmen's Compensation Law. When A. F. L. president Samuel Gompers (1850–1924) died, Green, with the backing of the United Mine Workers president, John L. Lewis (1880–1969), was elected to head the A. F. L. However, by 1935 a split had occurred between Lewis and Green over whether workers should be organized by crafts or by industries. Lewis, favoring the latter system, formed the Committee for (later Congress of) Industrial Organizations (C. I. O.), initiating a long and bitter struggle between the two giant labor groups. Despite Green's quarrels with Lewis and his lack of aggressiveness in dealing with management, the A.F.L. grew substantially in membership under his direction. Green, who in 1930 was awarded the Roosevelt Memorial Associa-

tion Medal for maintaining industrial peace, set forth his views on the labor movement in *Labor and Democracy* (1939). Three years after Green's death in 1952, the A. F. L. and the C. I. O. agreed to merge.

H

HARDING, Warren Gamaliel (1865–1923). The 29th President of the United States, Harding was a bewildered Chief Executive who once confided to a friend, "I knew this job would be too much for me." He died unexpectedly on the eve of the disclosure of a number of scandals, including the notorious **Teapot Dome** (*see*). Born in Blooming Grove, Ohio, Harding studied at Ohio Central College, and when 19, he moved to Marion. There, he and some friends purchased the bankrupt Marion *Star,* which prospered as the town's population increased. In 1891, Harding married Florence Kling de Wolfe (1860–1924), an heiress and a widow who was extremely ambitious. A Republican, he served in the state senate (1899–1903) and as lieutenant governor (1904–1905) but was defeated for governor in 1910. Harding's handsome features and talent for public speaking had attracted the attention of political boss **Harry M. Daugherty** (*see*), who later said, "He looked like a President ought to look." Daugherty and Harding's wife pushed him into running for the Senate in 1914, and Harding was elected by a substantial margin. As a Senator, Harding made many friends but did little else. He was not present for half of the roll calls and did not sponsor any important legislation. Under Daugherty's skillful management, however, he was kept in the political limelight and was recognized as a dark-horse possi-

bility for the Republican Presidential nomination in 1920. Harding was selected in a smoke-filled room by party leaders who wanted a candidate amenable to their suggestions. As one of them, Senator Frank B. Brandegee (1864–1924), said afterward, "Harding is no world-beater, but he's the best of the second-raters." Harding waged a "front porch" campaign, receiving visitors at his home in Marion and saying as little as possible. He defeated **James M. Cox** (*see*) with a plurality of more than 7,000,000 votes and an electoral vote of 404 to 127. Fully cognizant of his intellectual shortcomings, Harding promised a "return to normalcy" and pledged to name the "best minds" in the nation to his cabinet. His appointments of **Charles Evans Hughes, Herbert Hoover,** and **Henry C. Wallace** (*see all*) fulfilled this pledge. However, Harding also appointed old political cronies such as Daugherty and Albert B. Fall (1861–1944) to the cabinet and other unqualified friends to various important positions. The Washington Conference to limit naval armaments, which concluded in 1922, was the one noteworthy achievement of the Harding administration. The United States, Great Britain, and Japan agreed to place the tonnage of capital ships in a ratio of 5–5–3. As the year 1923 began, rumors of scandal were rife in Washington. Congressional investigations, involving several executive departments, were imminent. Meanwhile, Harding's love affair with Nan Britton (born 1896) was becoming public knowledge, and he paid for her to travel to Europe to quiet the gossip. That same year, a book appeared purporting to trace Harding's ancestry to a black great-grandmother and a grandmother of mixed races. It was promptly confiscated by the

Justice Department. Harding died in San Francisco of a blood clot that reached his brain on August 2, 1923, while returning from a trip to Alaska. A year later, it was revealed that he had been duped into transferring certain oil reserves from the navy to the Department of the Interior, an act that resulted in the scandal known as the Teapot Dome. Rumors then developed that Harding's death had been the result of suicide or even a mercy killing by his wife in order to avoid the scandal. The fact that Mrs. Harding had not permitted an autopsy and that she had returned to the White House and burned Harding's private papers added to the speculation. In 1927, Nan Britton published *The President's Daughter,* in which she claimed that Harding was the father of her eight-year-old daughter. Unlike the rumors about the manner of his death, this story has been substantiated by some historians.

HASSAM, Childe (1859–1935). Hassam was a leading American impressionist painter. He left his native Massachusetts in 1883 to travel and paint in Europe. Later, he spent three years studying art at the Academie Julian in Paris (1885–1888). Returning to the United States in 1889, Hassam started a studio in New York City. There, he associated with other artists painting in the impressionistic style. The vibrating colors and vigorous brush strokes characteristic of his work made him a leader in the movement. He became a member of "The 10," a group of American painters that included such well-known artists as J. Alden Weir (1852–1919) and John Henry Twachtman (1853–1902), who came together for an exhibition in 1898. During his stay in New York, Hassam painted numerous impressionistic street scenes (*see*

p. 1118). In 1897, he visited England for further study, but his style never changed. Unsympathetic to painters of a more modern style, he referred to them as his "contemptuaries." In his later years, Hassam painted scenes of New England, particularly its coast and villages. After 1915, he also began to do etchings. His better known paintings include *Summer Sea, Aphrodite,* and *Evening Bells*.

HAYS, William Harrison (1879–1954). Will Hays served as Postmaster General (1921–1922) during the administration of **Warren G. Harding** (*see*) and later was head of the so-called Hays Office (1922–1945), a moralistic movie-industry committee that censored motion pictures. Hays, who was born in Indiana, graduated from Wabash College in 1900. He became a lawyer in the same year and was also active in local Republican politics before he reached the age of 21. Quickly rising in the ranks of the party, Hays was chairman of the Republican State Central Committee from 1914 to 1918. He also headed the Indiana State Council for Defense during World War I and then presided over the Republican National Committee from 1918 to 1921. In that year, President Harding appointed Hays Postmaster General. As a member of Harding's cabinet, Hays never enjoyed popular trust because he was considered a political manipulator. In 1922, he became president of the Motion Picture Producers and Distributors of America. As such, 12 years later, Hays was responsible for putting into effect a set of motion-picture censorship rules known as the Hays Code. Leading film makers voluntarily subscribed to it in order to control the release of "immoral" movies. Hays served for five years as an adviser to

the industry after stepping down as president of the organization in 1945.

HEMINGWAY, Ernest (1899–1961). A rugged individualist who loved traveling, sports, and adventure, "Papa" Hemingway was one of the most influential and popular novelists to come out of World War I (*see p. 1161*). The Illinois-born writer began his literary career in 1917 as a reporter for the Kansas City *Star.* Eager for action, he left the newspaper to become a volunteer ambulance driver for the Red Cross in France in 1918. He later enlisted in the Italian infantry and was seriously wounded. Hemingway's experiences in Italy supplied him with the background material for *A Farewell to Arms* (1929), a novel reflecting his generation's disillusion with the glory of war. In 1919, he joined the staff of the Toronto *Star* and returned to Europe two years later as a foreign correspondent, settling in Paris. There his friends were other Americans who had chosen to live abroad, including the poets Gertrude Stein (1874–1946) and Ezra Pound (1885–1972). About 1923, Hemingway devoted himself almost entirely to writing fiction. His first successful novel, *The Sun Also Rises* (1926), is based on the aimless wanderings of the expatriates he encountered in Paris. Following the publication of *A Farewell to Arms,* Hemingway wrote two books of nonfiction, *Death in the Afternoon* (1932)—a study of bullfighting—and *Green Hills of Africa* (1935)—an account of big-game hunting. These books reflected his lifelong interest in the themes of courage, action, violence, and death and were written at a time when Hemingway traveled and hunted extensively. In 1937, he published *To Have and*

Have Not, a novel about the Depression. That same year, he went to Spain as a correspondent to cover the Spanish Civil War (1936–1939). Out of this experience came his only full-length play, *The Fifth Column* (1938), and his longest and one of his most famous novels, *For Whom the Bell Tolls* (1940). During the next decade, Hemingway wrote little fiction but was active as a correspondent in World War II. In 1950, his *Across the River and into the Trees* appeared but received poor reviews. However, it was followed two years later by *The Old Man and the Sea,* a story of an elderly fisherman's struggle with a marlin. Acclaimed as a masterpiece, the novella earned Hemingway the Pulitzer Prize for fiction in 1953 and was mentioned in his award of the Nobel Prize for literature in 1954. In it, Hemingway expressed his philosophy that for man, life is a losing battle in which personal dignity and stoic courage are of prime importance. Hemingway's reputation as a writer rests in good part on his prose style. His unemotional, terse, essentially colloquial writing has been much imitated. The novelist has been highly praised for his many short stories, among them "The Killers" and "The Snows of Kilimanjaro." After many years of ill health, Hemingway died from a self-inflicted gunshot wound at his home in Idaho. His posthumously published works include *A Moveable Feast* (1964), *The Wild Years* (1967), and *Islands in the Stream* (1970).

HOOVER, Herbert Clark (1874–1964). A renowned engineer and humanitarian, Hoover served a single term of office as the 31st President of the United States during the Great Depression. Like most leaders of business and government, he had not anticipated the economic panic that followed the stock-market crash in October, 1929. "In no nation," he had said in the spring of 1929, "are the fruits of accomplishment more secure." His efforts to revive the economy during his Presidency were largely unrewarded. A Quaker, Hoover was born at West Branch, Iowa, and grew up in Oregon. After graduating from Stanford in 1895, he embarked on a mining and engineering career, working in Australia, China, Africa, Egypt, Latin America, and Russia and eventually establishing offices in London, New York, and San Francisco. When World War I began, Hoover, who was by then a wealthy man, was appointed chairman of the American Relief Commission. In this capacity, he oversaw the evacuation of more than 150,000 American citizens from Europe. Hoover next headed (1915–1919) the Commission for Relief in Belgium, which supplied food and clothing to millions of people in Europe. He also served ably as United States Food Administrator (1917–1919) under President **Woodrow Wilson** (*see*) and worked on many other war-relief projects. As Secretary of Commerce (1921–1929) under Presidents **Warren G. Harding** and **Calvin Coolidge** (*see both*), Hoover enhanced his reputation as a public servant by fighting unemployment and promoting internal improvements, including the building of Boulder Dam (now called Hoover Dam) on the Colorado River in Arizona. When Coolidge retired in 1928, Hoover was nominated to head the Republican Presidential ticket. Using the slogan "Prosperity is just around the corner," he decisively defeated the Democratic candidate, **Alfred E. Smith** (*see*). Polling 6,000,000 more votes than his opponent, Hoover received 444 electoral votes to

Smith's 87. Within less than a year after succeeding Coolidge (*see p. 1127*), Hoover found himself in the midst of an ever-growing economic panic. With little success, he tried to combat "unjustified fear" and restore confidence in the economy. He initiated a public-works program and appointed commissions to make recommendations. The President's difficulties were compounded by diminishing foreign trade, financial crises in other nations, Japanese belligerence in the Far East, which threatened American interests, and the 1932 "Bonus March" on Washington, D.C., by disgruntled veterans. Hoover at first counted on the

Herbert Hoover

economy to right itself. By 1932, however, he was willing to back such forms of government intervention as the Reconstruction Finance Corporation, which was created to lend money to faltering businesses. The Hoover administration also extended aid to hard-pressed farmers through the Federal Farm Board and backed federal home-loan banks. However, by 1932 unemployment stood at more than 12,000,000, and Hoover's decisive defeat at the polls by Franklin D. Roosevelt (1882–1945) came as no surprise. During his many years in retirement after 1932, Hoover wrote *The Challenge to Liberty* (1934), *The Basis of Lasting Peace* (1945), and *The Ordeal of Woodrow Wilson* (1958). His *Memoirs* were published in three volumes in 1951 and 1952. The former President twice headed the Hoover Commission (1947–1949 and 1953–1955), which was set up to study the organization of the executive branch of the government. He died at the age of 90 on October 20, 1964.

HOUSE, Edward Mandell (1858–1938). "Colonel" House was the closest adviser to President **Woodrow Wilson** (*see*) and played a crucial role in American foreign relations during World War I and in the ensuing Paris Peace Conference that resulted in the **Treaty of Versailles** (*see*). His most outstanding achievement was in persuading the Allies to accept an armistice agreement with Germany based primarily on Wilson's Fourteen Points (*see pp. 1099–1100*). Born in Texas, House was active in Texas Democratic politics from 1892 until 1904 and got his nickname from Governor James S. Hogg (1851–1906), for whom he worked as an adviser. In 1912, House helped Wilson, whom he had first met the previous year, to gain the Democratic Presidential nomination by winning the support of Southern politicians and getting William Jennings Bryan (1860–1925) to back Wilson against **Champ Clark** (*see*). The two rapidly developed a deep friendship, and the Colonel helped Wilson, who called him his "alter ego," to select his cabinet. House's main interest was foreign affairs, and while in Europe in the spring and summer of 1914, he tried to prevent the outbreak of war. After hostilities began in Europe in August, 1914, House made two trips—in 1915 and 1916—to Paris, London, and Berlin in an attempt to convince the belligerents to accept an American-mediated peace. With America's entry into the conflict on April 6, 1917, House became Wilson's chief representative at conferences to coordinate the American war effort with Allied needs. During this phase of the war, he prepared policies for the eventual peace terms. As Wilson's representative, he secured an armistice based, for the most part, on the Fourteen Points by threatening the Allies that the United States would make a separate peace treaty with Germany. House subsequently served as member of the American peace commission at the Paris negotiations, but because of Wilson's decision to attend the conference in person, he did not have the same degree of authority he had formerly enjoyed. The President apparently resented House's realistic acceptance of compromises on the Fourteen Points, and after Wilson left for home on June 28, 1919, the two men never saw each other again. In 1921, House published *What Really Happened at Paris,* which he wrote with the historian Charles Seymour (1885–1963).

HUGHES, Charles Evans (1862–1948). A distinguished lawyer and the holder of many public offices, Hughes was both the Republican and the Progressive candidate for the Presidency in 1916 and had gone to bed on election night believing that he was elected. When the returns from California finally came in early the next morning, his Democratic opponent, **Woodrow Wilson** (*see*), had won by nearly 600,000 votes. Hughes' last and most important office was that of Chief Justice of the Supreme Court (1930–1941). Born in upstate New York, he graduated from Brown University in 1881 and from Columbia Law School three years later. He first received public notice in 1905 when he was counsel for a committee of the New York State legislature investigating gas companies. The following year, he won national recognition when he served as counsel for a similarly sponsored investigation of abuses in the insurance business. As Republican governor of New York (1907–1910), Hughes established two public-service commissions and secured the enactment of various labor laws and government reforms. In 1910, he resigned the governorship to serve as an Associate Justice of the Supreme Court. He left the Court in 1916 to run for the Presidency. After his defeat, Hughes resumed the practice of law until 1921, when President **Warren G. Harding** (*see*) appointed him Secretary of State (1921–1925). His main achievement in this office was at the Washington Conference of 1921–1922, where he secured the first successful limitations of naval armament. Hughes subsequently served as a member (1926–1930) of the Hague Tribunal and as a judge (1928–1930) of the World Court, both at The Hague in the Netherlands. He was named Chief Justice of the Supreme Court in 1930 by President **Herbert Hoover** (*see*). Hughes generally maintained a middle position between the conservatives and the liberals on the Court and tried to interpret the Constitution so as to make it fit the needs of the day. Although many of his decisions were progressive in spirit, he ruled against some of the New Deal measures of President Franklin D. Roosevelt (1882–1945). In 1935, for example, he received the Court's unanimous support when he ruled unconstitutional the National Industrial Recovery Act of 1933, which was designed to reduce unemployment and coordinate business and industry. In 1937, Hughes successfully blocked Roosevelt's plan to reorganize the Court. He retired in 1941.

I

INSULL, Samuel (1859–1938). Insull was a public-utility magnate whose billion-dollar empire collapsed overnight during the Great Depression. The London-born financier came to America in 1881. Hired by Thomas A. Edison (1847–1931) as his private secretary, Insull became president of the Chicago Edison Company in 1892. By 1907, he controlled all of Chicago's electric utilities, as well as its transit system. Through various mergers, Insull extended his interests into neighboring states. In 1912, he organized a vast interlocking directorate that eventually controlled nearly one-eighth of America's electricity. He then expanded his utility holdings to

include gas and steam plants. At the height of his power, Insull was a director of 85 companies and chairman of the board of 65 of them. His holdings were valued at $3,000,000,000. However, the financier overextended himself, and in 1932 his empire collapsed. When three of his largest companies went into receivership, investors lost $700,-000,000. Insull himself fled to Greece and later to Turkey. He was extradited to America in 1934. That same year, he was tried on charges of embezzlement and mail fraud but was acquitted. At his death, he was $14,000,000 in debt.

IZZIE and MOE. Izzie and Moe were government agents whose antics and achievements in enforcing prohibition during the Roaring Twenties were widely publicized. Soon after prohibition went into effect on January 16, 1920, gin mills and speakeasies opened all over the nation. At that time, Isadore Einstein

(1880?–1938), a fat, jolly, almost bald postal clerk in New York City, was having trouble supporting his family of seven on his salary and decided to obtain a job as an enforcement officer. He won admission to his first speakeasy by admitting he was a federal agent—the doorman thought he was being funny. Izzie soon convinced his long-time friend, Moe Smith (dates unknown), a taller, not as roly-poly cigar-store owner, to join him, and thereafter they worked as a team. In five years, they confiscated 5,000,000 bottles of liquor valued at $15,000,000 and made more than 4,000 arrests that resulted in convictions 95% of the time. Izzie and Moe were successful because of their ingenious ways of gaining admission to speakeasies that were on the lookout for federal agents. On one winter evening, for example, Izzie stood outside a speakeasy in his shirt-sleeves until he was red with cold. Moe then carried him inside, begging a drink for his friend. They often staged their raids for the convenience of reporters. One Sunday, accompanied by newsmen, Izzie and Moe made 71 raids in a little more than 12 hours. The publicity irked their superiors, who encouraged them to resign. In November, 1925, Izzie and Moe turned in their badges and began successful careers in insurance.

J

JOLSON, Al (1888–1950). A singer and actor, Jolson starred in the first talking picture, *The Jazz Singer,* in 1927. The Russian-born entertainer, whose real name was Asa Yoelson, came to America about 1895. The son of a rabbi, he first planned to become a cantor (religious singer) but turned to a

Fedora-clad Izzie and Moe pose with one of their "finds"—an illegal still.

theatrical career when he got a job as an 11-year-old extra in a New York stage play, *Children of the Ghetto*. He later traveled around the nation in vaudeville, minstrel shows, and circuses. While on tour in 1909, Jolson sang his first "mammy" song in blackface. The rendition established his reputation in the theater. During the next two decades, he starred in a series of plays, including *La Belle Paree* (1911), *Honeymoon Express* (1913), *Robinson Crusoe, Jr.* (1916), *Bombo* (1921), and *Big Boy* (1925). In 1927, Jolson made his first film, *The Jazz Singer,* which was also the first full-length talkie. He subsequently appeared in other films, had his own radio show after 1932, and became a film producer in 1944. Songs Jolson popularized include *April Showers, Swanee,* and *Mammy.* Two films were based on his life, *The Jolson Story* (*1946*) and *Jolson Sings Again* (*1949*).

K

KELLOGG–BRIAND PACT.
Signed by 15 nations on August 27, 1928, the Kellogg-Briand Pact was designed to outlaw war as an instrument of national policy. On April 6, 1927—the 10th anniversary of America's entry into World War I—the French foreign minister, Aristide Briand (1862–1932), asked the United States to sign a treaty outlawing war with France. Public opinion in America strongly favored acceptance. However, Frank B. Kellogg (1856–1937), United States Secretary of State, foresaw complications in an agreement made only with France, and he suggested that all nations sign such a pact. Initially, 13 other nations, including Germany, Italy, and Japan, agreed to the terms. Signed in

Paris, the Pact of Paris, as it was officially known, was written very simply and contained just three articles. The nations that signed condemned war and pledged to settle all future disputes "by pacific means." The treaty was very popular in the United States and was ratified by the Senate on January 15, 1929, with only one dissenting vote. Kellogg received the Nobel Peace Prize in 1929, largely because of his promotion of the pact. Despite the fact that 62 nations eventually signed the agreement, it proved to be meaningless. For example, Japan invaded Manchuria in 1931, and five years later Italy invaded Ethiopia without formally declaring war. Moreover, the only way of enforcing the pact's terms was through world opinion.

L

LEWIS, Sinclair (1885–1951).
The first American to receive the Nobel Prize for literature, Lewis satirized the American middle class. He was born and raised in Sauk Centre, Minnesota, a small town that later served as a model for his most successful books. Lewis graduated from Yale in 1908. For the next 12 years, he supported himself as a journalist and editor and wrote several novels. With the publication of *Main Street* in 1920 and *Babbitt* in 1922, Lewis established himself as a major American novelist. Both novels satirized the cultural poverty of small-town America and small-town Americans. The name Babbitt came to mean a smug, middle-class American whose values were shallow. Lewis' next novel, *Arrowsmith* (1925)—a sympathetic study of an idealistic medical scientist—was always his favorite. *Arrowsmith* was awarded the Pulitzer Prize for

fiction in 1926, but Lewis refused to accept it because he believed it had been awarded for the book's "wholesome atmosphere," not its literary merit. *Elmer Gantry* (1927), an indictment of Midwestern evangelism, and *Dodsworth* (1929), a study of wealthy Americans in Europe, preceded Lewis' Nobel Prize in 1930. He later published many more novels, but none of them approached the quality of his earlier works. Of these, *It Can't Happen Here* (1935), which warned of the dangers of fascism, is perhaps the best known. For a while, Lewis wrote and acted in plays, without notable success in either venture. His personal life was saddened by two divorces and the death of one of his sons in World War II. Always a heavy drinker, Lewis eventually lost most of his friends and died in a clinic in Rome.

LIE, Jonas (1880–1940).
This Norwegian-born artist departed from traditional landscape painting by choosing such subjects as industrial structures, harbors, and shipyards (*see p. 1129*). Lie decided to move to the United States in 1893. After graduating in 1897 from the Ethical Culture School in New York City, he went to work as a textile designer in Plainfield, New Jersey. Determined to pursue a painting career, Lie studied at night at the National Academy of Design and the Art Students League in New York. In 1900, he submitted his first canvas, *The Gray Day,* to the National Academy and had it accepted by the jury. Soon, Lie's paintings were being exhibited regularly. In 1912, he became an associate member of the National Academy. When the Panama Canal was being built between 1904 and 1914, Lie interpreted the historical significance of the occasion in a series of 12 paintings. Serving as presi-

dent of the National Academy from 1934 until 1939, Lie reorganized the jury of selections and extended the geographical representation of new members.

LLOYD GEORGE, David (1863–1945). Prime Minister Lloyd George, who headed the British delegation to the Paris Peace Conference in 1919 (*see p. 1103*), had won a general election the previous year with such slogans as "Make Germany Pay." He demanded that the defeated Berlin government pay heavy reparations. A Welshman by birth, Lloyd George was elected as a Liberal to Parliament in 1890 and served for 54 years. He was minister of munitions and then minister of war during World War I before becoming prime minister of a coalition government in December, 1916. At the end of the long and costly war, the British people and Lloyd George himself wanted vengeance. Only belatedly—after the peace talks began with President **Woodrow Wilson,** French Premier **Georges Clemenceau,** and Italian Premier **Vittorio Orlando** (*see all*)—did Lloyd George realize the possible consequences of a harsh treaty. He urged a cut in the proposed reparations and the admission of Germany to the League of Nations. However, Wilson and Clemenceau refused to consider Lloyd George's proposals, and the **Treaty of Versailles** (*see*) was signed in June, 1919. A Conservative revolt led to his ouster as prime minister in 1922, although he continued to serve in Parliament. Lloyd George was made a peer shortly before his death, but he did not live to take his seat in the House of Lords.

LODGE, Henry Cabot (1850–1924). As Senate majority leader and chairman of the Foreign Relations Committee, Lodge was instrumental in preventing America's ratification of the **Treaty of Versailles** (*see*). A wealthy Bostonian by birth, he received the first Ph.D. degree granted by Harvard College in political science in 1876. The following year, Lodge published *Life and Letters of George Cabot,* a biography of his great-grandfather (1752–1823), a leading Federalist who had served in the United States Senate. His other biographies include *Alexander Hamilton* (1882), *Daniel Webster* (1882), and *George Washington* (1888). Lodge first entered politics in 1879, when he was elected to the state legislature (1880–1881). He served six years (1887–1893) in the House of Representatives before being elected to the Senate in 1893. Lodge was a friend of Theodore Roosevelt (1858–1919), and when Roosevelt became President in 1901, he was one of his key advisers. A conservative party-line Republican, Lodge considered himself most competent in the field of international relations. In 1912, he introduced a resolution in the Senate that has since become known as the Lodge Corollary to the Monroe Doctrine. Its effect was to warn Asiatic powers such as Japan, which was then trying to lease a Mexican bay, not to go beyond ordinary trade relations with the nations of Central and South America. Lodge achieved national prominence only after he became the acknowledged leader of the opponents of the Treaty of Versailles. In addition to being a bitter political enemy of President **Woodrow Wilson** (*see*), Lodge sincerely believed that membership in the League of Nations would hamper the ability of the United States to respond in a crisis. Lodge wrote 14 reservations, which he succeeded in attaching to the treaty by a majority vote. The reservations were designed to limit the League's authority over American actions. Wilson was unwilling to compromise and asked loyal Democrats to vote against the treaty in that form. In November, 1919, the Senate rejected both the treaty with Lodge's reservations and the treaty as Wilson wanted it. Lodge then secretly engaged in negotiation with Democrats, trying to work out reservations they would accept. Senator **William Borah** (*see*),

Henry Cabot Lodge

who opposed the League in any form, threatened to call for Lodge's resignation as majority leader. Unwilling to have a fight within his own party, Lodge agreed to drop his negotiations. His version of the treaty again failed to pass the Senate in March, 1920. Lodge's defense of his actions was contained in a book published posthumously, *The Senate and the League of Nations* (1925). His grandson, former Senator Henry Cabot Lodge, Jr. (1902–1985), was the Republican Vice-Presidential candidate who was defeated in the 1960 election.

LOWELL, Abbott Lawrence (1856–1943). A political scientist and educator who was president of Harvard University for 24 years, Lowell was chairman of a special commission that upheld the guilty verdict in the **Sacco-Vanzetti case** (*see*). Born in Boston, Lowell was the brother of the poet Amy Lowell (1874–1925). He graduated from Harvard, then still a college, in 1877 and from Harvard Law School three years later. After practicing law in Boston for the next 17 years, Lowell became a lecturer in political science at Harvard. He was elevated to a full professorship in 1900. Succeeding Charles William Eliot (1834–1926) as president of Harvard in 1909, Lowell began to make fundamental changes in the institution's academic policies. Opposing the then current tendency toward overspecialization, Lowell revised the undergraduate curriculum to ensure that all students would receive a liberal education, as well as specialized courses. He also introduced to Harvard the tutorial method of study and the "house system," which was modeled after the British system of "inner colleges." As an administrator, Lowell was responsible for enlarging Harvard's physical facilities, quintupling its endowment, doubling the student enrollment, and opening the Schools of Business Administration and Education. In 1927, Massachusetts Governor **Alvan T. Fuller** (*see*) appointed Lowell to head the commission investigating whether the murder trial of anarchists Nicola Sacco (1891–1927) and Bartolomeo Vanzetti (1888–1927) had been fair. The panel upheld the original verdict of first-degree murder, and as a result the defendants were exe-

cuted. In his lifetime, Lowell received many honorary degrees, advocated the United States' entry into the League of Nations, and wrote many books on government.

LUSITANIA. The sinking of the British vessel *Lusitania* by a German submarine off the coast of Ireland in 1915 was a major factor in turning American public opinion against Germany after World War I had broken out in Europe. Launched in 1906, the 40,000-ton *Lusitania* was a luxurious passenger liner. The unarmed Cunard Steamship Company vessel sailed out of New York Harbor on May 1, 1915, with 1,250 passengers, including 179 Americans. Her cargo included 4,200 cases of small-arms ammunition. Three months earlier, the German government had proclaimed a war zone around the British Isles, warning that all Allied ships would be attacked. The day of the *Lusitania*'s departure, the German Embassy in Washington, D.C., published advertisements in New York newspapers announcing that Americans who traveled in this war zone on British or Allied ships went "at their own risk." By the afternoon of May 7, the *Lusitania* was 10 miles off Old Head of Kinsale, Ireland, when it was sighted by the German submarine *U-20*. The sub fired a single torpedo. Eighteen minutes later, a second explosion within the vessel ripped the *Lusitania* apart and she sank. In all, 1,198 people were lost, including 128 Americans. The sinking created an immediate furor in the United States. As the New York *Nation* wrote, "The torpedo that sank the *Lusitania* also sank Germany in the opinion of mankind." Pro-German sentiment among Americans evaporated, and pressure mounted on President **Woodrow**

Wilson (*see*) to declare war. Instead, he dispatched three notes of protest to Berlin. The first, on May 13, demanded that Germany disavow the sinking, make reparations, and cease its unrestricted submarine attacks. The second protest, sent on June 9, demanded a specific pledge. Secretary of State William Jennings Bryan (1860–1925), fearing that the second note would lead to war with Germany, had declined to sign it and resigned his cabinet post. Wilson's third note, on July 21, declared that any further submarine attacks would be regarded as "deliberately unfriendly." Finally, in May, 1916—a year after the sinking of the *Lusitania*—the German government pledged that it would not attack any more passenger or merchant ships without warning. Peace was thus temporarily preserved.

M

McADOO, William Gibbs (1863–1941). As Secretary of the Treasury (1913–1918), McAdoo directed the financing of World War I. He was born in Georgia to a wealthy family that lost its money as a result of the Civil War. Admitted to the bar in 1885, McAdoo practiced in Chattanooga, Tennessee, until 1892, when he opened a law office in New York City. There, McAdoo organized the Hudson and Manhattan Railroad Company, which raised $4,000,000 to build the first tunnel (1904) under the Hudson River, connecting New York City with New Jersey. McAdoo was an early supporter of **Woodrow Wilson** (*see*), and following Wilson's election in 1912, was named Secretary of the Treasury. He was instrumental in 1913 in securing passage of the Federal Reserve Act, which reorganized the na-

William G. McAdoo

tion's banking system, and served as the first chairman of the Federal Reserve Board. In 1914, he married the President's daughter, Eleanor Wilson (1889–1967). During World War I, McAdoo successfully promoted four Liberty Loans, which collected more than $18,000,000,000 to help pay the costs of the war. He also established a war-risk insurance law, which was later extended to life insurance for members of the armed forces. Named director general of railroads in December, 1917, McAdoo increased the efficiency of railroads by consolidating terminal facilities, standardizing equipment, shutting down little-used lines, and discouraging passenger travel. He resigned from the cabinet shortly after the Armistice to resume his law practice. McAdoo was a prominent contender for the Democratic Presidential nomination in 1920, but the party chose **James M. Cox** (*see*) instead. Four years later, his supporters and those of **Alfred E. Smith** (*see*) were deadlocked and the party chose a compromise candidate, **John W. Davis** (*see*). McAdoo, who had moved to Los Angeles, served one term in the Senate (1933–1939) before retiring from politics.

MOONEY, Thomas. *See* **Walsh, Frank.**

O

ORLANDO, Vittorio (1860–1952). Orlando, who headed the Italian delegation to the Paris Peace Conference in 1919 (*see p. 1103*), had been promised territorial concessions by the Allies in secret treaties. He arrived in Paris determined to see that the promises were made good by the other participants—President **Woodrow Wilson,** French Premier **Georges Clemenceau,** and British Prime Minister **David Lloyd George** (*see all*). Orlando entered politics in 1888 and held various cabinet posts before becoming the premier of Italy in 1917. At the peace conference, he sought implementation of the secret Treaty of London (1915), which promised Italy the Austro-Hungarian province of Dalmatia in what is now Yugoslavia. In addition, he demanded that Fiume, an Italian-

Vittorio Orlando

inhabited seaport on the Adriatic held by Austria-Hungary, be turned over to Italy. When Wilson made a direct appeal to the Italian people to renounce their claims, Orlando was so angry that he left the conference. He returned a month later when the Italian Parliament gave him a vote of confidence. However, the peace treaties signed with the defeated Central Powers failed to include Italian objectives, and Orlando resigned. Later, he was an early supporter of Benito Mussolini (1883–1945), but in 1925 he resigned from Parliament in protest over some of Mussolini's policies. In 1948, Orlando was elected to the Senate, and backed by leftist elements, he ran unsuccessfully for president of Italy that same year. He remained in the Senate until his death.

P

PAGE, Walter Hines (1855–1918). Named ambassador to Great Britain in 1913, Page opposed the strict neutrality policy of President **Woodrow Wilson** (*see*) and favored strong American support of the Allies. Born in North Carolina, Page was a newspaper editor and free-lance writer until 1883, when he secured control of the Raleigh *State Chronicle.* However, his crusades for reforms in agriculture, education, and industry were not popular in the South, and his paper was not a financial success. Page turned to magazine editing, working first for *Forum* (1890–1895) and then for the *Atlantic Monthly* (1896–1899). In 1899, he became a partner in the publishing house of Doubleday, Page & Company, and a year later he founded *The World's Work,* a magazine devoted to politics, and edited it until his appointment as ambassador 13 years later. Prior to the outbreak of World War I in Europe, Page did much to improve Anglo-American relations. Wilson was so pleased with his work that he obtained funds privately to allow Page, who had some personal financial problems, to remain at his post. After the war broke out, however, serious disagreements developed. Page was furious when the United States did not break diplomatic relations with Germany immediately after the sinking of the *Lusitania* (*see*) in May, 1915. He offered to resign in November, 1916, and waited a month without receiving a reply from Wilson. Wilson could not get the man he wanted to replace Page, and so he refused to accept his resignation. Page was not even certain that the **Zimmermann note** (*see*)—a German plot with Mexico against the United States—would convince Wilson to enter the war. After America entered the conflict in April, 1917, Page was effective in securing Anglo-American military and financial cooperation. A kidney infection forced him to resign in August, 1918, and he died two months later.

PALMER, Alexander Mitchell (1872–1936). Known as a progressive Democrat, Attorney General Palmer ruined his political career when he conducted a series of flagrantly illegal raids in 1919 and 1920 against immigrants who were allegedly radicals or Communists. Born of Quaker parentage in Moosehead, Pennsylvania, Mitchell graduated from Swarthmore College in 1891 and two years later began practicing law. A champion of the labor cause, he was elected to the House of Representatives for three terms (1909–1915). Palmer campaigned for **Woodrow Wilson** (*see*) in 1912. Despite his Quaker con-

victions, he supported World War I, in which he served as Alien Property Custodian and confiscated $600,000,000 worth of enemy property. In 1919, Wilson appointed Palmer his Attorney General. Postwar unrest during that same year included 3,600 labor strikes, race riots, and bomb scares, which a large segment of the American public attributed to a Communist conspiracy to take over the government. Palmer, meanwhile, reorganized the Justice Department, creating a special General Intelligence Division headed by J. Edgar Hoover (1895–1972), who later became director of the Federal Bureau of Investigation. Palmer, who hoped to be nominated by the Democratic Party to succeed Wilson, finally yielded to popular pressure to "do something" about the Bolshevik threat after his own home had been bombed and the Senate had censured him for not taking any action against subversives. Palmer decided to enforce the part of the immigration code that outlawed anarchism and punished all violators with deportation. On November 7, 1919, federal agents of the Justice Department conducted roundups of Russian immigrants in several cities and arrested about 450 persons, of whom 249 were deported to their homeland two weeks later. As a result of the so-called Palmer Raids, the Attorney General became a national hero. On January 2, 1920, Palmer next sent out his men, armed with 3,000 blank deportation warrants, on what was one of the largest mass arrests in the nation's history (*see p. 1155*). About 5,000 suspects in 33 cities were rounded up in detention centers. At this point, Palmer began to be denounced for disregarding the civil rights of his prisoners, and several investigations ensued. As evidence mounted, he was

accused of abandoning the due process of law in favor of illegal acts. The fear of the Communist menace was simultaneously dying down, and although Palmer had bragged that 2,720 of those picked up in the raid would be deported, in the end 4,000 suspects were released and only 556 were deported. In 1921, Palmer was accused of misusing his office by the Senate Judiciary Committee, but he denied any guilt. Fallen into disrepute, Palmer dashed his political hopes in an unsuccessful bid for the Democratic nomination in 1920 and spent the remainder of his life in obscurity.

PERSHING, John Joseph (1860–1948). One of America's most famous generals, "Black Jack" Pershing was commander in

John J. Pershing

chief of the **American Expeditionary Force** (*see*) in World War I. Pershing graduated from West Point in 1886. He took part in several campaigns against the

Indians before being transferred in 1895 to the Tenth Cavalry, a black regiment. His experiences with black troops made him their champion from then on and earned him the nickname "Black Jack" which remained with him the rest of his career. During the Spanish-American War, Pershing, then teaching at West Point, used his influence in order to go to Cuba with the Tenth Cavalry. He led it in the charge up San Juan Hill on July 1, 1898. Pershing first gained national attention while serving in the Philippines (1899–1903). He commanded campaigns against the Moros, tribesmen who were opposed to the American occupation. His success won praise from President Theodore Roosevelt (1858–1919), who in 1906 promoted him to the rank of brigadier general over 862 senior officers. In 1916, President **Woodrow Wilson** (*see*) ordered Pershing to lead a force of 12,000 men into Mexico to "pursue and disperse" bandits led by Pancho Villa (1877–1923), who had raided an American garrison in New Mexico. For almost a year, the American force engaged in a futile pursuit, but Pershing won praise for his patience and courage. In May, 1917, shortly after America entered World War I, Pershing was appointed commander of the American Expeditionary Force (A. E. F.) and supervised the organization of American troops. The British and French were dubious about the abilities of the untried Americans, but Pershing, backed by Wilson, insisted upon a separate and independent United States Army. Early in 1918, Marshal Ferdinand Foch (1851–1929) of France was named Allied commander. Pershing, however, insisted that the A. E. F. remain a tactical entity, and Foch reluctantly approved. On September 12, 1918, the A. E. F. and

six French divisions—in all 665,000 men—launched an offensive against the Saint-Mihiel salient, which had been in German control for four years. A day later, the salient was taken, at a cost of 7,000 American casualties. However, 15,000 German prisoners and 200 square miles of French territory had been taken, thus establishing the A. E. F.'s effectiveness. At the request of Foch, Pershing then moved his troops 60 miles for the Meuse-Argonne offensive (*see p. 1097*). The Allied forces outnumbered the Germans eight to one, but the battle raged until an armistice was signed on November 11, 1918. German casualties numbered 100,000, while the Americans suffered 117,000 (*see pp. 1100–1101*). Pershing objected to the Armistice, saying, "They don't know they were beaten in Berlin, and it will all have to be done all over again." In 1919, Pershing was made General of the Armies, the highest rank held by anyone since George Washington (1732–1799). He served as Army Chief of Staff for three years before retiring from active duty in 1924. His memoirs, *My Experiences in the World War,* won the Pulitzer Prize for history in 1932.

R

REED, James Alexander (1861–1944). This Ohio-born politician served three consecutive terms (1911–1929) as a United States Senator from Missouri. His family had moved from Ohio to Cedar Rapids, Iowa, in 1864. There, he received a public-school education and attended Coe College. After studying law, he was admitted to the Iowa bar in 1885. Two years later, he established his practice in Kansas City, Missouri. Reed served as prosecuting attorney (1898–

1900) for Jackson County before resigning to become mayor (1900–1904). He was elected to his first Senate term in 1910. Reed opposed prohibition and the United States' membership in the League of Nations. Although a Presidential hopeful in 1928, he lost the Democratic nomination to **Alfred E. Smith** (*see*). He did not seek a fourth term in the Senate that year, choosing instead to resume his legal career in Kansas City.

RICHTHOFEN, Manfred von (1892–1918). Germany's most famous air ace in World War I, Baron von Richthofen was credited with downing a record 80 Allied planes, more than any other pilot on either side. Richthofen was born into a landowning family in Breslau. His father was an army officer. Richthofen joined the cavalry as a lieutenant in 1912. After the outbreak of war in 1914, fighting in trenches made the cavalry obsolete, so he transferred to the infantry and won the Iron Cross, Germany's highest military honor. Restless, Richthofen switched to the air force in 1915 and served as an observer on the Russian and French fronts. The following year, he became a fighter pilot and subsequently commanded a squadron nicknamed the Flying Circus for its aerial antics (*see p. 1117*). Richthofen himself was called the Red Knight because he flew a red Fokker triplane and was known for his chivalry in battle. On September 17, 1916, he scored his first kill. Before his own death on April 21, 1918, he claimed 79 more Allied planes. That day, his triplane was shot down over Amiens, France, by a Canadian pilot, Captain Roy Brown (*see p. 1107*). Richthofen's sister, Frieda, was the wife of the famous English novelist D. H. Lawrence (1885–1930).

RICKENBACKER, Edward Vernon ("Eddie") (1890–1973). America's top air ace in World War I, Eddie Rickenbacker later became one of the leaders in the commercial airline field. Born in Columbus, Ohio, Rickenbacker went to work at the age of 11 in a glass factory. Later, he studied automotive engineering by mail, and by the age of 20 he was a successful car salesman. To promote the sale of his cars, he raced in the Indianapolis "500" in 1911 and 1912 and then turned to automobile racing exclusively. Rickenbacker joined the army when America entered World War I in 1917. He was assigned to chauffeur Colonel William Mitchell (1879–1936), one of the first promoters of an American air force. Mitchell approved his application for flight training despite the fact that Rickenbacker was over the age limit. He reached the front in early 1918, and before the Armistice, downed four observation balloons and 22 planes—the highest aircraft tally of any American pilot. Rickenbacker wrote of his experiences in battling the squadron led by the German ace Baron **Manfred von Richthofen** (*see*) in *Fighting the Flying Circus* (1919). After the war, Rickenbacker founded an automobile manufacturing company, which went bankrupt in 1925. He later paid off all the company's debts himself. After serving as an airline executive in several companies, Rickenbacker in 1938 managed to secure control of Eastern Airlines, which he built into a major airline. During World War II, Rickenbacker went on numerous special missions to inspect airforce facilities. In October, 1942, his plane was forced down in the Pacific Ocean. Rickenbacker spent 23 days in a life raft before he and six others were rescued. His book, *Seven Came Through* (1943), recounts this experience. Rickenbacker served as chairman of the board of Eastern Airlines from 1953 until his retirement in 1963. His autobiography, *Rickenbacker,* was published in 1968.

RITCHIE, Albert Cabell (1876–1936). This lawyer served four terms as the Democratic governor of Maryland (1920–1936). Born in Richmond, Virginia, Ritchie moved with his family to Maryland when he was a young boy, and he spent most of his life there. He graduated from Johns Hopkins University in 1896, received a law degree from the University of Maryland in 1898, and subsequently established a successful law practice. Ritchie earned a state-wide reputation in 1912 as people's counsel for the State Public Service Commission. After engaging in a long legal battle with utility companies, he won reduced gas and electricity rates for Maryland consumers. This achievement figured in Ritchie's election as attorney general of Maryland in 1915. He remained in this office until 1919, except for a six-month leave during World War I, when he served as general counsel to the nation's War Industries Board. Ritchie was elected to his first term as governor of Maryland in 1919. He carried out many reforms, including raising his state's educational and public-health standards. Ritchie's popularity among voters and his efficient record led to his reelection three successive times. During the 1920s, Ritchie was a firm believer in states' rights. He opposed prohibition on the ground that it was unconstitutional. By the middle of the decade, he had abandoned his earlier reform philosophy and had allied himself with the conservative wing of the Democratic Party. Because his conservatism appealed to Southerners and business interests and because his antiprohibition stand was attractive to urban interests, Ritchie was mentioned as a Presidential contender at the Democratic National Convention in both 1928 and 1932. However, by 1932 the prohibition issue had become overshadowed by the Depression, and Ritchie's support died away. His fifth bid for the governorship of Maryland in 1935 resulted in his only defeat.

ROGERS, William Penn Adair ("Will") (1879–1935). Often called the cowboy philosopher, Will Rogers was a humorist and actor whose satiric wit delighted audiences for nearly 30 years.

CULVER PICTURES

Will Rogers

He was born in the Indian Territory (now part of Oklahoma) of Cherokee extraction. Proud of his Indian blood, Rogers quipped, "My ancestors didn't come over on the *Mayflower*—they met the boat." Rogers spent his childhood on his father's ranch, where he became an expert roper. After briefly attending Kemper Military School in Missouri (1897–1898), Rogers quit to work as a cowboy in the Texas Panhandle. In 1902, the restless young man traveled to Argentina and then took a cattle boat to South Africa. There he joined a Wild West show as a roping artist. He later toured Australia with the company. Returning to America in 1904, he made his New York debut the following year. When Rogers spoke for the first time on stage in 1905, he discovered that his informal chatter with the audience was more entertaining than his rope tricks. He later incorporated news of the day into his patter and poked fun at Presidents, stuffed shirts, political parties, and fads. Rogers made his first appearance on Broadway in *The Wall Street Girl* in 1912 and starred three years later in *Hands Up*. He was a star of the *Ziegfeld Follies* from 1916 to 1925. Regardless of the role, he always "played his natchell self." He first appeared in the movies in 1918 and also became a popular radio commentator, as well as the author of a syndicated newspaper column. Rogers published several books, including *Letters of a Self-Made Diplomat to His President* (1927). He was killed with his pilot, Wiley Post (1900–1935), when their monoplane crashed near Point Barrow, Alaska, on a flight to the Orient.

RUTH, George Herman ("Babe") (1895–1948). At the Baseball Centennial Dinner held in July, 1969, to celebrate the 100th

Babe Ruth

anniversary of professional baseball, Babe Ruth was named the greatest player in the history of the sport. The stocky, barrel-chested slugger was born in Baltimore and attended St. Mary's Industrial School for underprivileged boys. In 1914, he was signed by the Baltimore Orioles of the International League. Before the end of the season, Ruth was sold to the Boston Red Sox of the American League. As a left-handed pitcher, he won 87 games and lost 44 in his five seasons as a pitcher with the Red Sox. In 1919, Ruth was shifted to the outfield to take advantage of his hitting ability. That year, he set a major-league record by hitting 29 home runs. At the end of the season, Ruth was sold to the New York Yankees for a reported $100,000 plus a $370,000 personal loan to the Red Sox owner. His hitting prowess and flamboyant personality immediately increased the attendance in New York (*see p. 1149*). Yankee Stadium, built in 1923, is still known as The House That Ruth Built.

The last of the 15 home runs that Ruth hit in World Series play was also his most dramatic. Playing against the Chicago Cubs in Wrigley Field in the third game of the 1932 series, Ruth came to bat in the fifth inning with the score tied, 4–4. After Charlie Root pitched a strike, Ruth pointed with his index finger to the grandstand, indicating that he would hit a homer there. Root, however, whipped another strike by him. Ruth then pointed with his bat in the same direction and this time knocked the ball into the grandstand. Near the end of his career in 1935, Ruth signed with the Boston Braves of the National League, but he did not complete the season. Three years later, he briefly served as a coach for the old Brooklyn Dodgers. In his more than 20 years in the major leagues, Ruth set or tied 76 records. His career total of 714 home runs in regular season play was surpassed only by Hank Aaron in 1974, and his 1927 season total of 60 was surpassed only after the number of games played in a season was increased. His lifetime batting average was .342. In 1936, Ruth joined Ty Cobb (1886–1961) as a member of baseball's Hall of Fame. Off the field, Ruth was well-known for his charity work, especially with children. Before his death, he established the Babe Ruth Foundation to aid underprivileged youth.

S

SACCO, Nicola. *See* **Sacco-Vanzetti case.**

SACCO–VANZETTI CASE. The trial and execution in Massachusetts of two Italian immigrants—Nicola Sacco (1891–1927) and Bartolomeo Vanzetti (1888–1927)—caused protests through-

Artist Ben Shahn depicted Sacco and Vanzetti in chains at their murder trial.

out the world, based on the belief that the two men had been convicted of murder because of their radical political views. Sacco and Vanzetti emigrated from Italy in 1908. They earned their living as a shoemaker and a fish peddler respectively. On April 15, 1920, a paymaster and a guard at a shoe factory in South Braintree, Massachusetts, were murdered and the company's $16,000 payroll stolen. Sacco and Vanzetti were arraigned as suspects because they were found carrying firearms, their car was linked to the robbery, and witnesses identified men of Italian appearance as the criminals. The arrests came at a time when anti-Communist sentiment was high in the nation. Sacco and Vanzetti lied about their activities on the day of the murders to avoid punishment for their political actions. At their trial, which began in May, 1921, in Dedham, Massachusetts, the publicized fact that the defendants were anarchists, draft dodgers, and labor agitators resulted in prejudiced behavior on the part of the presiding judge and prosecuting attorney. Although Sacco and Vanzetti had witnesses to prove that they were not at the scene of the crime, and no evidence of the stolen payroll could be traced to them, they were declared guilty of first-degree murder in July, 1921, and sentenced to die. For the next six years, Sacco and Vanzetti appealed their case and sought a new trial. Public outcry against the obvious travesty of justice resulted in anti-American demonstrations. In addition, petitions were signed by prominent people urging their release, and a Sacco-Vanzetti defense committee raised funds on their behalf. However, by 1927, all legal means had been exhausted. In July of that year, the governor of Massachusetts appointed **Abbott Lawrence Lowell** (*see*), president of Harvard; Samuel W. Stratton (1861–1931), president of the Massachusetts Institute of Technology; and Judge Robert Grant (1852–1940) to review the case. They concluded that the trial had been fair and upheld the verdict. With clemency denied, the accused, maintaining their innocence to the end, were electrocuted on August 22, 1927. Ballistic studies in 1961 showed that it was Sacco's gun that had fired the fatal bullets, though no proof has ever been uncovered that he wielded it on that occasion. The Sacco-Vanzetti case has become a popular theme in American literature and is the subject of at least eight novels, 144 poems, and six plays, the most famous being *Winterset* (1935) by Maxwell Anderson (1888–1959).

SINCLAIR, Harry. *See* **Teapot Dome.**

SMITH, Alfred Emmanuel (1873–1944). The Democratic Presidential candidate in 1928, Smith was the first Roman Catholic to be nominated by a major party. The grandson of Irish immigrants, Smith was raised on New York's Lower East Side and went to work at the age of 13 to support his widowed mother. He made friends with a saloonkeeper, who also happened to be the Tammany Hall district leader. With his help, Smith entered politics and in 1903 was elected to the state legislature (1904–1915), becoming speaker of the Assembly in 1913. After serving as sheriff (1915–1917) of New York County and president (1917) of the New York City Board of Aldermen, Smith was elected governor in 1918. He was defeated for reelection in the Republican landslide of 1920 but won the governorship again in 1922, 1924, and 1926. During his total of eight years in office, Smith proved an excellent administrator and a progressive on questions of power regulation, labor, and social reforms. He also opposed prohibition. At the Democratic National Convention of 1924, Smith's name was placed in nomination by Franklin D. Roosevelt (1882–1945) in a speech in which Roosevelt called Smith "the Happy Warrior." Supporters of Smith and **William G. McAdoo** (*see*) deadlocked the convention for 103 ballots, and the nomination finally went to **John W. Davis** (*see*). However, Smith won the nomination in 1928 on the first ballot. The campaign that year centered on the personalities of Smith and the Republican candidate, **Herbert Hoover** (*see*). Smith was criticized for his unsophisticated speech and informal manners, his identification with a big city political machine, his "wet" position on prohibition, and his religion. Despite his strong defense of the separation of church and state, many voters believed that if Smith were elected the pope would move to Washington. Smith received the electoral votes of only eight states, and his total popular vote of 15,000,000 was 6,000,000 votes shy of what Hoover received. It was the first time since the Reconstruction Era that a Democrat failed to carry the entire South. Smith's active political career ended when he lost the 1932 nomination to Roosevelt. He subsequently opposed New Deal policies, and as a founder of the anti-Roosevelt Liberty League, supported Republican candidates in 1936 and 1940. Most of his time, however, was spent in business. He served as president of the company that owned and operated the Empire State Building from 1929 until his death.

SULLIVAN, Mark (1874–1952). A popular newspaper columnist and social historian, Sullivan was the author of *Our Times— The United States, 1900–1925* (1926–1935), a six-volume account of American politics, manners, and mores in the early 20th century from the point of view of a political conservative. Pennsylvania-born Sullivan received his bachelor's (1900) and law (1903) degrees from Harvard and then embarked on a wide-ranging journalistic career. He was on the staff of the *Ladies' Home Journal* (1903–1905), *Collier's Weekly* (1905–1919), the New York *Evening Post* (1919–1924), and after 1924, the New York *Tribune*. Sullivan began as an investigative muckraking journalist, attacking abuses in such areas as the patent-medicine industry. Later, he devoted himself to defending conservative Republican policies in his syndicated column in the *Tribune*. He was a friend and adviser of both Theodore Roosevelt (1858–1919) and **Herbert Hoover** (*see*). Sullivan published his autobiography, *The Education of an American,* in 1938 and remained active as a journalist until his death.

T

TEAPOT DOME. The illegal use of public oil lands in Wyoming and California for private profit —made possible by corruption within the administration of President **Warren G. Harding** (*see*)— has come to be known as the Teapot Dome scandal. The notorious episode was brought to light in 1923 after an extensive investigation headed by Senator **Thomas J. Walsh** (*see*) of Montana. During the administrations of Presidents William Howard Taft (1857–1930) and **Woodrow Wilson** (*see*), substantial petroleum reserves at Teapot Dome, Wyoming, and Elk Hills, California, were set aside for the use of the United States Navy. In 1921, Secretary of the Navy Edwin M. Denby (1870–1929), following President Harding's instructions, transferred the administration of the two naval-reserve areas to the Department of the Interior, headed by Albert B. Fall (1861–1944). The following year, Fall secretly leased the Teapot Dome reserve to the Mammoth Oil Company of Harry F. Sinclair (1876–1956), and the Elk Hills reserve to the Pan-American Petroleum Company of Edward L. Doheny (1856–1935). In return, Sinclair "lent" Fall nearly $300,000 in cash and negotiable securities, and Doheny furnished the Secretary of the Interior with another $100,000 "loan"—in cash, in a "little black bag." In the trials that followed these revelations by the Walsh committee, Fall in 1929 was convicted of taking bribes, fined $100,000, and sentenced to a year in jail. Sinclair and Doheny were acquitted of fraud charges, but Sinclair drew a nine-month jail term for jury tampering and contempt of the Senate. Neither Navy Secretary Denby nor the unwitting President Harding— who had died on August 2, 1923 —were criminally implicated in the scandal. The illegal oil leases were invalidated by the Supreme Court in 1927.

TREATY OF VERSAILLES. The Treaty of Versailles was the most important of the five treaties that ended World War I, but it did not secure a lasting peace. The peace conference opened in Paris on January 18, 1919. The drafting of the treaty was largely the work of the so-called Big Four—President **Woodrow Wilson** of the United States, Prime Minister **David Lloyd George** of Great Britain, Premier **Georges Clemenceau** of France, and Premier **Vittorio Orlando** of Italy (*see all*). The final draft was a compromise reached after long and difficult negotiations (*see pp. 1101–1103*). Wilson achieved his major aim, the inclusion of

The Treaty of Versailles redrew the map of Europe at Germany's expense.

the League of Nations Covenant in the treaty. Defending its importance, he said, "The settlements may be temporary, but the processes must be permanent." The treaty required Germany to abandon 25,000 square miles of territory in Europe, to yield all overseas possessions, to reduce her military services to a point where she was defenseless, to permit Allied occupation of the Rhineland, and to accept guilt for the war. Germany was to pay an initial $5,000,000,000 in reparations, and a reparations commission was established to determine the total sum, which

was set at $33,000,000,000 in 1921. When first presented with the Treaty of Versailles in May, 1919, German officials protested its terms. They correctly claimed that it did not adhere to Wilson's Fourteen Point peace program, which had been the basis of the armistice. However, realizing they had little choice, they signed the treaty on June 28, 1919, at the Hall of Mirrors in the Versailles Palace. Subsequent treaties with the other former warring nations recognized the independence of seven new nations in Europe—Yugoslavia, Czechoslovakia, Poland, Lithu-

ania. Estonia, Latvia, and Finland. Wilson returned to the United States to face opposition to the Treaty of Versailles. Senator **Henry Cabot Lodge** (*see*) and others objected particularly to the League of Nations, and the treaty was eventually defeated (*see pp. 1103–1104*). The Treaty of Versailles was declared in force on January 10, 1920, following ratification by the other Allied powers and Germany. Legally, the war did not end for the United States until July 2, 1921, when Congress passed a joint resolution declaring the end of hostilities.

TUNNEY, James Joseph ("Gene") (1897–1978). In one of the most famous prizefights in sporting history, Gene Tunney defeated **Jack Dempsey** (*see*) for the heavyweight boxing championship of the world on September 23, 1926, in Philadelphia. More than 120,000 people paid nearly $2,000,000 to view the contest. In a return match in Chicago a year later, Tunney, a superb athlete and a "scientific" boxer, retained the title, surviving a controversial seventh-round knockdown to win a 10-round decision. Many fans thought he would have lost the fight if Dempsey had quickly retired to a neutral corner. The referee did not begin the "long count" until Dempsey had done so. Born in New York City, Tunney began boxing in local gyms as a youth. While serving in Paris with the Marine Corps during World War I, he won the light-heavyweight title of the **American Expeditionary Force** (*see*). Tunney returned to the United States in 1919 and went into professional boxing. He captured the world light-heavyweight crown three years later from Battling Levinsky. That same year, Tunney was dethroned by Harry Greb, but he regained his title from

Greb in 1923. In 1926, having lost only once in 60 professional bouts, Tunney relinquished the light-heavyweight championship to fight in the heavyweight division. His two victories over Dempsey made him undisputed king of the heavies, and he retired as undefeated champion in 1928. Tunney then began a successful business career, interrupted by World War II, when he was director of physical fitness for the United States Navy.

V

VALENTINO, Rudolph (1895–1926). The "Great Lover" of the silent screen, Valentino was a film star best remembered for his role in *The Sheik* (see p. 1148). The Italian-born actor immigrated to the United States in 1913. After working as a gardener and dancer, he joined a musical-comedy company. The company left him stranded in San Francisco, and he went south to try his luck in Hollywood. There, he found bit parts

Rudolph Valentino as the Sheik

in the movies. In 1921, he was given the starring role in *The Four Horsemen of the Apocalypse,* a war film. The movie established the slick-haired actor as the Latin lover of the decade. After his role in *The Sheik* in 1921, Valentino was idolized by women the world over. His other films included *The Conquering Power, Camille, Moran of the Lady Letty,* and *Blood and Sand.* When he died in 1926, nearly 30,000 heartbroken fans mobbed the funeral parlor in New York City.

VANZETTI, Bartolomeo. *See* **Sacco-Vanzetti case.**

VON RICHTHOFEN, Manfred. *See* **Richthofen, Manfred von.**

W

WALLACE, Henry Cantwell (1866–1924). As Secretary of Agriculture (1921–1924), Wallace tried to bring farmers out of the agricultural depression that followed World War I. Although unsuccessful, he did reorganize the Department of Agriculture and establish several new bureaus. Born in Illinois, Wallace learned the printer's trade while attending school and helping on the family farm. After graduating from Iowa State Agricultural College in 1892, he joined his father, Henry Wallace (1836–1916), in purchasing a dairy magazine. Renamed *Wallaces' Farmer,* it became one of the nation's outstanding farm journals. After his father's death, Wallace moved up from associate editor to editor in chief. In 1921, President **Warren G. Harding** (*see*) chose Wallace as his Secretary of Agriculture (*see p. 1120*). At that time, farmers were gripped in an agricultural depression that had pushed their purchasing power below the

prewar level. In an effort to improve their situation, Wallace persuaded Harding to call a conference to formulate a plan for farm relief. However, the President's National Agricultural Conference, held in January, 1922, did little more than offer a few legislative recommendations and coin a slogan, "Equality for Agriculture." It never made clear how such equality could be established. Wallace also tried to protect the farmer from being further squeezed by the middleman. He opposed the transfer of marketing functions to the Department of Commerce, a move strongly urged by the Secretary of that department, **Herbert Hoover** (*see*). Wallace believed that his department should not only retain that control but also develop improved methods of marketing. An avid conservationist, Wallace also fought the corrupt Department of Interior to retain the Forest Service in the Agriculture Department. His son, Henry A. Wallace (1888–1965), became Secretary of Agriculture during the first two administrations of President Franklin D. Roosevelt (1882–1945) and was Vice-President during Roosevelt's third term.

WALSH, Francis Patrick ("Frank") (1864–1939). During his long career as a lawyer and public official, Walsh promoted the causes of organized labor, civil liberties, and other reform movements. Born in St. Louis, Walsh grew up in Kansas City, Missouri. He left school at an early age to support his family. After studying law at the office of a local attorney, he was admitted to the Missouri bar in 1889. Entering local politics as a Democrat about 1892, Walsh worked for a succession of progressive measures in his state during the first decade of the

20th century. In 1908, he organized what became known as the Kansas City Board of Public Welfare, which brought him into national prominence. In 1913, President **Woodrow Wilson** (*see*) appointed Walsh chairman of the United States Commission on Industrial Relations, and for the next two years he traveled across the nation, investigating the causes of conflict between labor and management and arousing public sympathy on labor's behalf. During World War I, Wilson named Walsh and former President William Howard Taft (1857–1930) cochairmen of the newly created National War Labor Board. Together, they heard 1,200 cases involving labor disputes and prevented many strikes. Following the war, Walsh agitated for Irish independence at the Paris Peace Conference of 1919 and in the United States, serving as counsel for the self-proclaimed Irish Republic. As one of the leading labor lawyers of the 1920s, he worked for the preservation of civil liberties, notably in his defense of the labor leader Thomas Mooney (1882–1942), who had been convicted of murder for his role in the fatal bombing at San Francisco's 1916 Preparedness Day Parade. Through Walsh's efforts, Mooney was pardoned in 1939. Walsh also tried unsuccessfully to prevent the executions in 1927 of the principals in the **Sacco-Vanzetti case** (*see*). In 1930, Franklin D. Roosevelt (1882–1945), then the governor of New York, appointed Walsh head of the State Power Authority, and later, when Roosevelt was President, Walsh's ideas on public power helped influence the development of the Tennessee Valley Authority, a federal agency that manages a complex waterpower, industrial, agricultural, and recreational system. When liberal lawyers formed the National Lawyers Guild in 1936 in protest over the conservative policies of the American Bar Association, Walsh became its first president. He resigned three years later because the association had not denounced Communist dictatorships and other totalitarian governments.

WALSH, Thomas James (1859–1933). A Democratic Senator from Montana who was one of the most capable and progressive-minded legislators of the early 20th century, Walsh is best remembered as the man who exposed the notorious scandal known as the **Teapot Dome** (*see*) in 1923. In 1922, as head of the Senate Investigating Committee, Walsh undertook a painstaking 18-month inquiry into alleged wrongdoing in the leasing of naval oil reserves in Wyoming and California to private interests. His findings uncovered one of the major episodes of corruption in the administration of **Warren G. Harding** (*see*). A native of Two Rivers, Wisconsin, Walsh practiced law for six years in the Dakota Territory after receiving his law degree from the University of Wisconsin in 1884. In 1890, he moved to Helena, Montana, where he gained a reputation as both a mining and a constitutional lawyer. He won election to the Senate in 1912 and served until his death (1913–1933). Consistently championing liberal legislation, Walsh was an early proponent of women's suffrage and of restrictions on child labor. He helped draft the Eighteenth Amendment, which established prohibition, and the Nineteenth Amendment, which gave women the right to vote—though he later backed the repeal of prohibition. Walsh also defended the right of farm groups and trade unions to be exempt from antitrust suits and vigorously supported President **Woodrow Wilson** (*see*) on such issues as the **Treaty of Versailles** (*see*), the League of Nations, the World Court, and limitations on military arms. He also spoke out strongly against the hysterical "Red hunt" conducted by Attorney General **A. Mitchell Palmer** (*see*) in 1919 and 1920. Walsh declined to accept the Democratic nomination for Vice-President on the ticket with **John W. Davis** (*see*) in 1924. In 1933, President-elect Franklin D. Roosevelt (1882–1945) named him United States Attorney General in his new administration. He died before he could take office.

WEEKS, John Wingate (1860–1926). This Republican politician served in both houses of Congress and was Secretary of War under **Warren G. Harding** (*see*). Weeks was born near Lancaster, New Hampshire, and graduated from Annapolis in 1881, but he was discharged from the navy in a layoff of personnel two years later. He subsequently worked as a surveyor. In 1888, Weeks entered the banking and brokerage business in Boston, eventually becoming a partner of the financial house of Hornblower & Weeks. After the Spanish-American War, in which Weeks patrolled the Massachusetts coast as part of his state's naval militia, he became involved in local politics and was elected as alderman-at-large in 1900 and as mayor three years later of the Boston suburb of Newton. Elected to the House in 1904, Weeks gave up his business connections to serve four terms as a Representative (1905–1913). He resigned upon his appointment to fill a vacant Senate seat. As a Senator, Weeks generally espoused traditional Republican views, although he voted for the Federal Reserve Act proposed by President **Woodrow Wilson** (*see*) in 1913. Weeks' opposition to prohibition and his vote against women's-suffrage amendments contributed to his defeat in the election of 1918. Two years later, during the Presidential campaign, Weeks was in charge of New York's Republican headquarters and won the admiration of Harding. The new President appointed him to his cabinet in 1921. He served as Secretary of War until 1925, when illness forced his retirement. During the 1925 controversy concerning the adequacy of the nation's air defenses, Weeks denied before a House investigating committee charges of "incompetency, criminal negligence, and almost treasonable administration" made by Colonel William "Billy" Mitchell (1879–1936).

WHEELER, Burton Kendall (1882–1975). Wheeler represented Montana in the Senate for 24 years, but he bolted the Democratic Party in 1924 to run for Vice-President on the Progressive Party ticket headed by Robert LaFollette (1855–1925). A native of Massachusetts and a graduate of the University of Michigan (1905), Wheeler practiced law in Butte, Montana, served in the state legislature (1911–1913), and was a federal district attorney (1913–1922) before his election to the Senate in 1922. He quickly established his reputation as a reformer by undertaking investigations that led to the uncovering of the **Teapot Dome** (*see*) scandal. He and LaFollette received only 4,831,-000 votes out of 29,000,000 cast in the 1924 election, and following their loss to **Calvin Coolidge** (*see*), Wheeler returned to the Democratic Party. He supported most of the New Deal legislation put forward by Franklin D. Roosevelt (1882–1945), but vigorously opposed Roosevelt's plan in 1937 to enlarge the Supreme Court (*see pp. 1253–*

1258). Then, as one of the leaders of the isolationist movement preceding World War II, Wheeler broke with Roosevelt completely. He attacked the Lend-Lease program as foreign policy designed to "plow under every fourth American boy." Wheeler was defeated in the 1946 primaries, and he returned to Montana to practice law.

WILHELM II (1859–1941). Described variously as a madman or a fool, Wilhelm was the kaiser (emperor) of Germany for 30 years and during World War I came to symbolize the enemy to most Americans (*see p. 1099*). A grandson of Britain's Queen Victoria (1819–1901), Wilhelm was born with a withered left arm, which some historians believe may have motivated his aggressive nature. In 1890, less than two years after he became emperor, he dismissed his chancellor, Otto von Bismarck (1815–1898). Bismarck's foreign policy had been based upon maintaining a balance of power between the nations of Europe, but Wilhelm launched a program to

strengthen Germany's armed forces, particularly the navy, and entered the race for colonies and foreign commercial markets. Such pronouncements as "We fear nothing or no one in this world" served to alarm much of the world. During the Boxer Rebellion in China in 1900, Wilhelm exhorted German troops to emulate the Huns in aggressiveness. When World War I began, Wilhelm was compelled by circumstances to let high-ranking military personnel run both the war and the government. However, as "Supreme War Lord," he approved all major policy decisions. In early October, 1918, the German military leaders realized they could not win the war, and on November 9

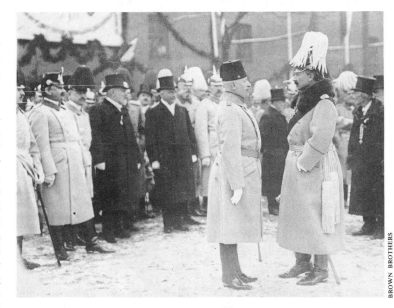

BROWN BROTHERS

Attired in a plumed helmet, Kaiser Wilhelm confers with a Turkish officer.

Field Marshal Paul von Hindenburg (1847–1934) advised Wilhelm to abdicate. President **Woodrow Wilson** (*see*) had previously indicated that he would not negotiate with Wilhelm. Wilhelm fled to the Netherlands on November 10, 1918, and he remained in exile there until his death. The Allies planned, in Article 232 of the **Treaty of Ver-**

sailles (*see*), to place him on trial as a war criminal. However, the Netherlands, which had remained neutral throughout the war, refused to extradite him.

WILSON, (Thomas) Woodrow (*Continued from Volume 12*). The man who had won reelection on the slogan "He kept us out of war" found that less than a month after his second inaugural he was asking Congress to formally declare war on Germany. On April 6, 1917, four days after his request, the United States entered World War I. President Wilson's greatest contribution in the ensuing two years was the formulation of idealistic war aims, known as the Fourteen Points, on which he later hoped to base the **Treaty of Versailles** (*see*). These were stated on January 8, 1918. Wilson said that peace would be based on six general points: open diplomacy, freedom of the seas, the removal of international trade barriers, the unbiased settlement of colonial claims, a drastic reduction in armaments, and the creation of a league of nations to preserve international peace and justice. The eight additional points dealt with specific territorial and political problems and settlements of immediate concern to the belligerents. On November 11, 1918, the Germans agreed to an armistice, largely because Wilson virtually assured them that the peace settlement would be based on his Fourteen Points. He personally headed the American delegation to the peace conference that met in Paris from January to June, 1919, thus becoming the first President to leave the United States while in office. Wilson, a Democrat, took with him advisers such as his close friend Colonel **Edward M. House** (*see*), but he made the mistake of not asking any Senators or Republican politicians to join the delegation—serious political errors, because the Senate would have to ratify any peace treaty he proposed and because the Republicans had won control of both houses of Congress in 1918. Although the Europeans hailed Wilson as the champion of democracy, he soon found himself at odds with the other representatives at the peace conference—**David Lloyd George** of Britain, **Georges Clemenceau** of France, and **Vittorio Orlando** of Italy (*see all*). The resulting treaty was a compromise measure that expressed a vindictive attitude toward Germany. Wilson's major successes were the inclusion in it of a covenant establishing the League of Nations and the modification of the harsh terms desired by the other Allies. However, when the treaty was finally presented to the Senate for ratification in July, 1919, it was opposed by many Senators—led by the Republican isolationist **Henry Cabot Lodge** (*see*)—who believed that membership in the League would result in too great an American involvement in European affairs and undermine United States sovereignty. By refusing to compromise, Wilson made it impossible to reach any agreement. On September 4, 1919, he left Washington, D.C., on a strenuous national speaking tour to promote popular support for ratification of the treaty. The strain was too much for him, and while in Pueblo, Colorado, on September 25—after 37 speeches in 29 cities—he collapsed from exhaustion. A severe stroke that followed a few days later when he was back in the capital partly paralyzed his left side. Wilson remained isolated from all politics for the rest of his term, while his wife, Edith Bolling Galt Wilson (1872–1961), virtually exercised the powers of Chief Executive. The Senate failed to ratify the treaty in November, 1919—and again in the following March—though Wilson was awarded the Nobel Peace Prize for his efforts that year. His successor, Republican **Warren G. Harding** (*see*), made it clear that the United States would never join the League of Nations and concluded a separate peace with Germany in 1921. "Tired of swimming upstream," Wilson died in his sleep on February 3, 1924.

Y

YORK, Alvin (1887–1964). The most popular hero of World War I, Sergeant York was credited with single-handedly killing 20 Germans and capturing 132 others and 35 machine guns. York was raised on a backwoods farm in his native Tennessee. When the United States entered the war, he requested exemption from active duty because of pacifist religious beliefs. Nonetheless, he was drafted and rose to become a sergeant in the 328th Infantry, 82nd Division. It was while fighting in the Argonne Forest on October 8, 1918, that York stormed the enemy positions on his own. He was subsequently awarded the Medal of Honor and the French Croix de Guerre. After the war, York returned to Tennessee and settled on a farm given him by the state. He later established the York Foundation for educating impoverished mountain children and became active in the world peace movement.

Z

ZIEGFELD, Florenz (1869–1932). "Flo" Ziegfeld was one of the great showmen and theatrical producers in the history of American entertainment. For

Pulchritude, not vulgarity, was the hallmark of Ziegfeld's famed chorus line.

24 years (1907–1931), he presented the annual *Ziegfeld Follies,* a spectacular musical revue—the first of its kind in America—that was noted for its beautiful girls and lavish costumes and staging. Ziegfeld was born in Chicago, the son of the founder of the Chicago Musical College. He began his career in show business by providing bands and other musical entertainment for the Chicago World's Fair of 1893, at the same time managing Eugene "Sandow the Great" Sandow (1867–1925), a professional strong man who became one of the fair's leading attractions. In 1896, Ziegfeld produced the first of his many plays, *A Parlor Match,* starring the comedienne Anna Held (1873?–1918), whom Ziegfeld married in 1897. However, it was his *Follies,* first staged in 1907, that brought him fame and riches. Besides stunning chorus lines and opulent settings, the *Follies* featured such comic talents as **Will Rogers** (*see*), Eddie Cantor (1892–1964), and W. C. Fields (1880–1946). Although Ziegfeld made ample use of the feminine form in his spectaculars— "Glorifying the American Girl" was his motto—he avoided vul-garity. Among his other successful productions were *Sally* (1920), *Show Boat* (1927), *Rio Rita* (1927), and *Bitter Sweet* (1929). Ziegfeld—part artist and part carnival barker—promoted his theatricals with as much advertising hoopla as he could muster. Divorced from Anna Held in 1913, Ziegfeld married the famous actress Billie Burke (1886–1970) the following year. His career took a sharp downturn when the Great Depression began in 1929, and he died in Hollywood three years later, having exhausted his huge personal fortune through extravagant living.

ZIMMERMANN, Arthur. *See* **Zimmermann note.**

ZIMMERMANN NOTE. Intercepted and decoded by British intelligence, the Zimmermann note solidified American public opinion against Germany and was an important factor leading to American entry in World War I on the side of the Allies. On January 17, 1917, British intelligence in London monitored and decoded a message from German Foreign Secretary Arthur Zimmermann (1864–1940) in Berlin to the German ambassador in Mexico. The ambassador was instructed to offer Mexico an alliance with Germany, if and when the United States abandoned her neutrality. In return, Mexico would receive New Mexico, Texas, and Arizona. Mexico was also to try to get Japan to abandon the Allied cause and join Germany. At the time, Mexico was in the midst of a revolution, and General **John J. Pershing** (*see*) was in northern Mexico with 12,000 troops, chasing the rebel leader Pancho Villa (1877–1923). The chief of British intelligence decided not to inform his government or the United States of the message. He did not want the Germans to know that their code had been broken unless it would bring America into the war. Then, in response to the resumption of unrestricted submarine warfare, President **Woodrow Wilson** (*see*) announced on February 3 the severance of diplomatic relations with Germany. By February 23, British intelligence decided that the timing was right, and the full text of the note was delivered to **Walter Hines Page** (*see*), the United States ambassador to Great Britain. Page immediately forwarded the note to Wilson. Because the telegram had originally been sent via the German ambassador in Washington, D.C., Wilson was able to verify its contents by checking with Western Union in the capital. On March 1, the telegram was made public. Pacifists and German sympathizers immediately charged that the telegram was a hoax, but Zimmermann admitted its authenticity on March 3. The threat of aggression on American soil meant that the war could no longer be viewed as an exclusively European fight, and on April 2, 1918, Wilson asked Congress for a declaration of war against Germany.

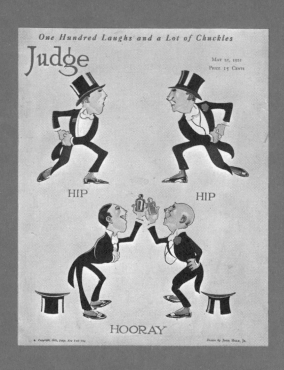